backyard wild birds
of the east and midwest

by vinson brown

illustrated by
rosinda holmes

ISBN 0-87666-412-5

Distributed in the U.S.A. by T.F.H. Publications, Inc., 211 West Sylvania Avenue, P.O. Box 27, Neptune City, N.J. 07753; in England by T.F.H. (Gt. Britain) Ltd., 13 Nutley Lane, Reigate, Surrey; in Canada by Clarke, Irwin & Company, Clarwin House, 791 St. Clair Avenue West, Toronto 10, Ontario; in Southeast Asia by Y. W. Ong, 9 Lorong 36 Geylang, Singapore 14; in Australia and the south Pacific by Pet Imports Pty. Ltd., P.O. Box 149, Brookvale 2100, N.S.W., Australia.
Published by T.F.H. Publications, Inc. Ltd., The British Crown Colony of Hong Kong.

INTRODUCTION

The main purpose of this book is to give the user a handy, reasonably-priced guide to the common birds found in backyards of the east, the midwest (as far west as Missouri and Minnesota), and the south of the United States (as far west as Louisiana), and most of southeastern Canada. The book also shows how such birds may be attracted to yards for greater enjoyment. In addition, the book describes and illustrates a number of less common land birds so that travelers into the wilder mountain areas, for example, can use it as an aid in bird identification. Thus the book is a fairly complete volume on the land birds (and a few of the shore birds) of the region covered.

To use this book, first learn to find bird types by shape in the helpful key on pages 4 and 5. The numbers in this key do not refer to page numbers; they refer to numbered bird illustrations and descriptions found in the book. Carefully study these key pages so you can picture the shapes of the bodies, heads, wings, bills, and tails of the various birds. Notice that some types of birds, like owls and bob-whites, have thick bodies, whereas others have thin or medium bodies. Hawks are best differentiated by carefully studying the wing and tail shapes. Long, thin bills are distinctive of the thrashers and mockingbirds, while short, stout bills are typical of the sparrows and finches; less specialized bills are found among thrushes, blackbirds, and orioles, that eat many kinds of foods, and short, thin bills are typical of warblers, gnat-catchers, and kinglets.

The birds with colors and color patterns that are the most useful in identification are shown in color in the back half of the book, while the more plain-looking birds are shown in black and white in the front half of the book. The book is built around these color plates and line drawings in such a way as to be most useful for the amateur bird watcher, so it is arranged somewhat differently from most bird books. The birds are kept so far as possible in their natural groups. But where a bird family, such as the flycatchers, is divided between the color plate section and the line drawing section of the book, the birds in each section are cross referenced by number. Carefully check these numbers, and the illustrations and descriptions to which they refer so you can picture in your mind the complete family of birds in your region. It is also suggested that a special mark be put in the front of the name of each bird that is found in the state or province where you live so you may quickly turn to the pictures and descriptions of the birds that live in your area.

Sex of birds illustrated is designated by the symbols ♂ for male and ♀ for female.

ILLUSTRATIONS OF FEEDING, WATERING AND HOME SITES

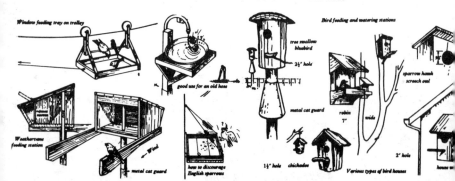

ATTRACTING, FEEDING AND HOUSING BIRDS

Attracting birds to your backyard successfully requires: 1. providing them with habitats and hiding places that they like; 2. giving them favorite food plants; 3. putting up feeding and watering stations; 4. providing them with good nesting sites.

HABITATS AND HIDING PLACES. Produce in your yard a variety of places (habitats) in which birds like to live and hide. A grassy place, a little pond with rushes around it, trees, clusters of bushes, rough hedges, a vine-covered fence or wall, all are good.

FOOD PLANTS. Good *trees* and *shrubs* include elderberries, white mulberry, blueberry, flowering crab, red cedar, nanny berry, barberry, coralberry, smooth sumac, Japanese yew, peppertree, and Asiatic sweetleaf.

Good *vines* include Virginia creeper, greenbrier, honeysuckles (especially good for hummingbirds), grapes, and matrimony vines.

Useful *herbs* are sunflowers, chicory, blazing star, and asters. Ask about these and other plants birds like at your neighborhood nursery.

FEEDING AND WATERING STATIONS. Some of these are illustrated on the opposite page. Be sure all are protected from cats and squirrels by metal sheets tacked around trunks or poles, or by hanging from wires. Attract birds first by putting food on stumps and rocks, later luring them to stands and cable trays. Favorite foods of birds are listed in the descriptions. Many, including bird seed, suet and insect mixes, can be obtained at pet stores. Hummingbird nectar feeders are also obtainable at pet stores.

GOOD NESTING SITES. Natural nesting sites you furnish by providing trees, hedges, vines, brush, rushes and clumps of high grass. Five general types of homes for birds are shown on the opposite page. Home preferences where known for each bird are given in the bird descriptions. You will be disappointed about birds using your bird houses unless you carefully watch where each kind of bird likes to live and place your bird house where that bird likes it to be. Rustic bird houses that look like tree stumps are especially good. Notice that most holes are placed high on the house with a resting place just below. Some birds, such as the swallows and martins, nest in groups. A line of hollow gourds, with proper size holes, hung from a beam, wire or branch are good for these.

The illustrations are from HOW TO MAKE A MINIATURE ZOO, by Vinson Brown, published by Little, Brown and Co., Boston, Massachusetts.

KEY TO BIRD SHAPES

Soaring Hawks 7-11

Vultures, 1-2

Accipiter Hawks, 4-6

Falcons, 12-14
Kites, 3

Bob-white, 17
Grouse, 15-16
Partridge, 18

Pheasant, 19

Doves, 88-90

Killdeer, 20

Nighthawks, 27

Owls, 29-36

Woodpeckers, 91-100

Kingfisher, 28

Hummingbirds
101-102

Flycatchers, 37-42,
105-109
Kingbirds, 103-104

Woodcock, 21
Common Snipe, 22

Swallows, 43-49
Martin, 49

Swifts, 43

Whip-poor-wills, 25
Chuck-will's Widow,
26

KEY TO BIRD SHAPES

Cuckoo, 23-24

Crow, 114
Raven, 113

Jays, 110-112

Shrikes, 117-118
Mockingbird, 58

Thrushes, 126-129
Robins, 125
Bluebirds, 131

Horned Lark, 42

Chickadees, 50-52
Titmouse, 53

Thrashers, 60
Mockingbird, 58
Catbird, 59
Pipit, 62

Nuthatches, 119-121
Creepers, 112

Gnatcatchers, 61

Wrens, 54-57

Vireos, 132-138
Kinglets, 123-124

Warblers, 139-175

Waxwings, 115-116

Orioles, 181-182
Blackbirds, 63-65
178, 180
Starling, 176
Meadowlarks, 177
Bobolink, 179

Grosbeaks, 189,
191-193
Crossbills, 196-197
Purple Finch, 190
Cardinal, 187
Tanagers, 183-184

Goldfinch, 195
Buntings, 87
185-186
Siskin, 194

Sparrows, 66-85
Juncos, 86
Towhees, 198
Dickcissel, 188

5

1. TURKEY VULTURE

4. GOSHAWK

adult

2. BLACK VULTURE

immature

3. MISSISSIPPI KITE

6. COOPER'S HAWK

5. SHARP-SHINNED HAWK

VULTURES, KITES, AND BIRD HAWKS

These birds and the hawks and falcons discussed next are meat or fish eaters. Some may be attracted to a yard by tying nets with fresh meat in them on tree branches.

1. TURKEY VULTURE *(Cathartes aura)*. Wingspread 6'. Breeds from northern Minnesota to western Connecticut and south to the Gulf of Mexico. Winters from the Ohio Valley and southern New Jersey south. *The small naked red head (black in young birds) is distinctive, as are the very large blackish wings, which are noticeably lighter on the flight feathers.* When soaring, which it does beautifully and for long periods, the turkey vulture holds its wings at an angle above the horizontal and at times tilts and rocks itself in a rather wobbly way.

2. BLACK VULTURE *(Coragyps atratus)*. Wingspread up to 5'. Resident in the southern United States and as far north as Missouri, Indiana, West Virginia, and Maryland. *The short square tail of this large black bird and its comparatively short and wide wings force it to fly with distinctively frequent and labored wing-flapping between short sails. The small naked head is black.* These birds often gather in numbers near butchering areas and garbage dumps.

3. MISSISSIPPI KITE *(Ictinia missisippiensis)*. Size up to 14" long. Summer visitor in Kansas, Missouri, and Tennessee (mainly southwest); resident in lower tier of southern states. *The black tail and very light pearly gray head, contrasting with the dark back, combined with the pale bands bordering the rear of the wings, quickly distinguish this species.* Kites often hover over a field or swamp, looking for snakes, lizards, mice, etc. The SWALLOW-TAILED KITE, *Elanoides forficatus*, of South Carolina and Florida to Louisiana swamps, is rarer, but easily identified by the long forked tail.

4. GOSHAWK *(Accipiter gentilis)*. Size up to 26" long; wingspread up to 4'. This and the following two hawks are Accipiters, or Bird Hawks, and are distinguished by having short broad wings and long tails; they are adapted to diving through branches after birds. Usually fly with short fast wing beats, followed by glide. The Goshawk breeds in wooded areas of Canada, south to the northern edge of the United States, but winters as far south as Virginia, Kentucky, and Missouri. *The large size, white stripe over eye, black blotch behind eye, and black crown are distinctive. The pale gray belly make the bird appear much lighter colored than its smaller relatives, discussed below.*

5. SHARP-SHINNED HAWK *(Accipiter striatus)*. 10-14" long. Breeds in wooded areas from Canada to the southern states; winter visitor and resident in United States. *The dark rusty barred breast distinguishes this small hawk from the Goshawk, but it is told from the Cooper's Hawk only by small size and square-tipped tail* (seen best when tail is folded). Very shrill "kay, kay, kay" call.

6. COOPER'S HAWK *(Accipiter cooperi)*. 14-20" long. Breeds and winters in same ranges as the preceding hawk. *Appears exactly like Sharp-shinned Hawk except for larger size and more rounded tail.* Both hawks have similar rapidly repeated screams, but the call of this species is hoarser. All three bird hawks rarely soar, but are noted for their silent, swift, and fierce attacking of birds, generally through foliage.

BUTEO HAWKS AND FALCONS

Buteos-flight silhouette

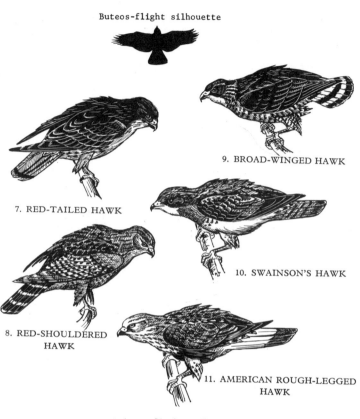

9. BROAD-WINGED HAWK

7. RED-TAILED HAWK

10. SWAINSON'S HAWK

8. RED-SHOULDERED
HAWK

11. AMERICAN ROUGH-LEGGED
HAWK

Falcons-flight silhouette

13. MERLIN or
PIGEON HAWK

14. KESTREL or
SPARROW HAWK

12. PEREGRINE FALCON

8

BUTEO HAWKS AND FALCONS

The following five buteo or buzzard hawks have distinctively broad, rounded tails and long, broad wings adapted to prolonged and usually circular soaring. Young hawks are often dark-streaked on their breasts.

7. RED-TAILED HAWK *(Buteo jamaicensis)*. 19-25″ long; wingspread up to 4½′. Breeds in open woodlands and brushlands from southern Canada to the southern states; winters as far north as Maine, Ohio, and Iowa. *Tail shows bright red upper surface.* Body chunky and wings unusually wide. A rasp-like, squealing scream "krce-rr-rr."

8. RED-SHOULDERED HAWK *(Buteo lineatus)*. 18-24″; wingspread up to 4½′. Breeds and winters much as preceding hawk. *Told by dark broad bands, separated by whitish lines, on tail both above and below, and the uniform reddish-brown and white banding on belly and breast.* Whitish translucent blotch on outer part of underwing is another identifying mark. Gives two-syllabled piercing "keeee-errr" whistle.

9. BROAD-WINGED HAWK *(Buteo platypterus)*. 14-19″ long; wingspread up to 3¾′. Breeds from southeastern Canada to the Gulf Coast in open woods, but winters from Florida south. Very similar to above bird in appearance from a distance, but adults have white and black-brown bands of equal size on tail, while both adults and young are recognized by the much chunkier body, shorter wings, and stubbier tail. The very high, shrill "pf-eee-weeeeee" whistle is plaintive in tone.

10. SWAINSON'S HAWK *(Buteo swainsoni)*. 19-22″; wingspread up to 4¼′. Breeds as far east as Minnesota and western Iowa; a migrant in the Mississippi Valley. *Most adults have a wide brown breast band; when flying, the whitish inner wing color contrasts sharply with the darker brownish of the outer wing feathers.* Like that of the Rough-legged Hawk, the brownish tail usually changes to white at the base. However, some individuals are light colored without the breast band, or are very dark in general color. For these the contrasting white and dark of the underwing is useful in identification. Plaintive, shrill "kreee-ee-ee!" whistle.

11. AMERICAN ROUGH-LEGGED HAWK *(Buteo lagopus)*. 19-24″; wingspread up to 4¾′. Winters from southern Canada to northern Texas, Louisiana, and North Carolina, generally in open areas. *The unusually long wings and tail are generally sharply-marked with black and white.* The light phase has a sharply contrasting heavy black band underneath the white tail, while the dark phase has a dark band shading more gradually into the whitish tail base. Light phases have distinctively contrasting black blotches on underwing elbows and a similar heavy black band across chest; dark phases have all dark ventral surfaces, dark inner wing linings, and white bases of flight feathers.

12. PEREGRINE FALCON *(Falco peregrinus)*. 15-20″; wingspread up to 3½′. This and following two birds are recognized as falcons by their distinctive long, pointed wings and long, narrow tails, as well as by very swift, steady wing-beats in flight. The Peregrine breeds from Canada to Louisiana and Georgia and winters over most of the United States. *Told by large size and heavy black "mustache-like" bars on cheeks.*

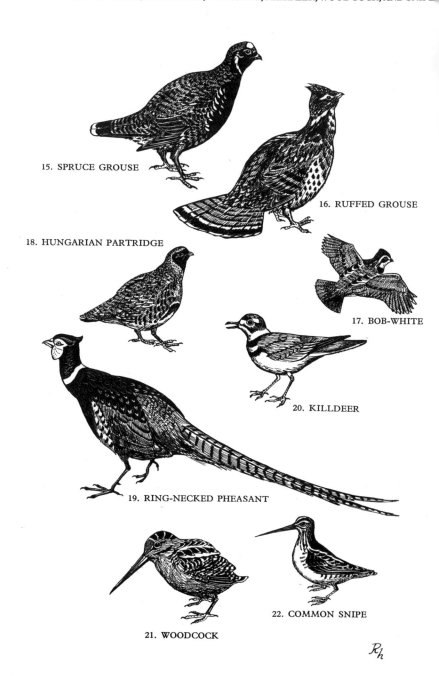

15. SPRUCE GROUSE

16. RUFFED GROUSE

18. HUNGARIAN PARTRIDGE

17. BOB-WHITE

20. KILLDEER

19. RING-NECKED PHEASANT

21. WOODCOCK

22. COMMON SNIPE

13. MERLIN or PIGEON HAWK *(Falco columbarius)*. 10-13½″; wing-spread up to 2⅓′. Breeds over most of the United States and the southern border of Canada; winters from Gulf States south. *The wide dark and light bands on tail are distinctive.*

14. KESTREL or SPARROW HAWK *(Falco sparverius)*. 9-12″; wing-spread up to 2′. Resident over most of eastern United States and southeast border of Canada. Frequents various habitats. *The only small hawk with a rufous-red back and tail.* Hovers frequently with rapidly-beating wings. The cry is a very rapid, shrill "kee-kee-kee" or "killy-killy-killy." Can be lured to bird house in a tree or under house eaves.

GROUSE, BOB-WHITE, PARTRIDGE, PHEASANT, KILLDEER, WOODCOCK AND SNIPE

15. SPRUCE GROUSE *(Canachites canadensis)*. 15-17″. Found in spruce forests in Canada and in jack pines and spruce of northern border of the United States. The general brown color above is set off by a *red mark behind the eye and a reddish-brown band at end of tail in males,* which is also blotched black and white below. Female is browner and thickly marked with bars. Male makes a fluttering, drumming sound with wings, not as loud or rolling as that of the Ruffed Grouse. Feeds on leaves, greens, berries, and insects.

16. RUFFED GROUSE *(Bonasa umbellus)*. 16-20″. Resident in Canada and south into Iowa, Missouri, Ohio, and down the Appalachian Mountains into Georgia and Alabama, frequenting brushy woods, often near streams. *If a large reddish-brown or gray-brown chicken-like bird suddenly springs into the air from the brush with a loud whirr, it is likely to be this bird.* The distinctive fan-shaped tail has a wide, black band near end. Male gives deep, booming, rolling sound with wings. Eats such things as leaves, twigs, catkins, and berries.

17. BOB-WHITE *(Colinus virginianus)*. 8-10½″. Found from southwest Maine and southern Ontario to the Gulf, mainly in farm or abandoned farming country. The small size, short bill, short tail, and explosive flight take-off are distinctive. *Male has white throat and white above-eye stripe, sharply contrasting with brown general colors.* Has clear ringing whistle with the sound "bob-white" often heard. Eats weed seeds, berries, and insects.

18. HUNGARIAN PARTRIDGE *(Perdix perdix)*. 12-14″. Found locally in several eastern states, particularly those of upper Mississippi Valley. *Distinguished by round gray body, short reddish-brown tail, and reddish-brown marks on under sides.* Gives a loud rasping "kah-whit, kah-whit" call. Eats grains, weed seeds, and berries.

19. RING-NECKED PHEASANT *(Phasianus colchicus)*. Male 32-36″; female 19-21″. Found in scattered farming areas in the more northern states and southern Ontario. *The very long, curved and pointed tail is distinctive;* male with bright red and violet-purple on head, white neck ring, and reddish colors on back and tail; female mainly brownish. Male gives loud, startling, double cry. Feeds on such plant parts as grains, weed seeds, and fruits.

20. KILLDEER *(Charadrius vociferus)*. 9-11". Breeds from southern Canada to the Gulf; winters, preferably in open areas, from southern Illinois and Long Island south. *The two sharply-marked, black, breast bands and the golden-red rump are characteristic.* Loud, shrill "kill-dee" call. Feed principally on insects.

21. WOODCOCK *(Philohela minor)*. 10-12". Breeds from southern Canada to the Gulf; winters from Ohio Valley and New Jersey south, frequenting swamps and thickets. *Thick body; neckless appearance; brown, leaf-patterned color, and the very long bill are distinctive;* wings rounded and short, giving whistling sound in flight. Male gives soft nasal "bzeep" call; also warbles, and wings produce a trilling sound. Eats mainly insects and worms, but some weed seeds.

22. COMMON SNIPE *(Capella gallinago)*. 10-11½". Breeds from Canada southward into Iowa, Illinois, and northwest Pennsylvania; winters from northern states south, preferring wet meadows and bogs. *The brown and white striped back and head, extremely long slender bill, stubby orange tail, and zig-zag flight are distinctive.* Produces rasp-like sound in flight. Feeds mainly on insects, worms, and seeds of aquatic plants.

CUCKOOS, WHIP-POOR-WILLS, NIGHTHAWK, AND KINGFISHER

23. YELLOW-BILLED CUCKOO *(Coccyzus americanus)*. 11-13". Breeds from southern Canada to the Gulf, Florida, and Mexico, in woods near streams; winters in South America. Olive-brown above; *the slim body, long, white-spotted tail, and the flash of reddish-brown in the wings in flight are characteristic.* Makes rapid gargling series of "ka, ka, ka, kaow-kaow-kowp" notes, or single "kaow." Eats insects.

24. BLACK-BILLED CUCKOO *(Coccyzus erythropthalmus)*. 11-12½". Breeds from southern Canada to North Carolina, Georgia, and Arkansas; winters in South America. *Similar to yellow-billed cuckoo, but has black bill, small red ring around eye, and much smaller tail spots.* Call of "cu-cu-cu" is distinctively grouped in series of three to five notes. Feeds on insects. Both cuckoos show a snake-like movement as they fly. Both might be attracted to robin-type open nest box in tree.

Goatsuckers. The following three species are wide-tailed, night or evening flying birds, with tiny feet and small bills, but large mouths lined on sides with hairs to trap moths and other insects in flight. Rarely attracted to robin-type bird houses.

25. WHIP-POOR-WILL *(Caprimulgus vociferus)*. 9-10". Breeds from southern Canada to northern Louisiana and northern Georgia; winters from the coast of South Carolina and the Gulf Coast south, generally in woodlands. Brownish and blackish, dead-leaf markings with reddish-brown suffusion above and *distinctive white throat mark; white edge to tail feathers in male,* Usually flies up from hiding place on ground to catch insect prey. Loud repeated "wheep-poor-weel" call.

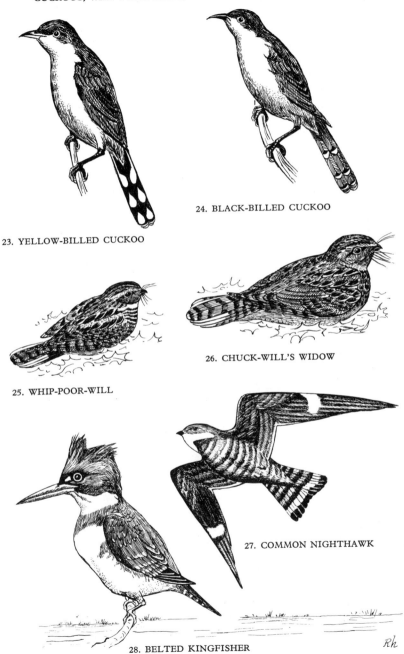

24. BLACK-BILLED CUCKOO

23. YELLOW-BILLED CUCKOO

26. CHUCK-WILL'S WIDOW

25. WHIP-POOR-WILL

27. COMMON NIGHTHAWK

28. BELTED KINGFISHER

Rh

26. CHUCK-WILL'S WIDOW (*Caprimulgus carolinensis*). 11-13″. Breeds in low-lying, usually damp land from Missouri, Ohio, and Maryland southward to Florida and the Gulf; winters from southern Florida south. Very similar to the whip-poor-will but larger, more brownish, and with *yellow-brown mark* instead of white *on throat*. Call sounds like "chuck-weels-widow," but weaker than whip-poor-will's call.

27. COMMON NIGHTHAWK (*Chordeiles minor*). 8-10″. Breeds from southern Canada and Newfoundland to the Gulf and Florida; winters in South America. *Told instantly by the long slim wings, swift erratic flight while after insects high in the air, and the bright white patches or bands across the wings that contrast with the dark gray or gray-brown colors.* Sometimes flies in daylight as well as at night. Gives nasal "pee-eek" or "pee-eent" call. Male drops from sky to make booming, whirring noise when courting female.

28. BELTED KINGFISHER (*Megaceryle alcyon*). 11-14″. Breeds from Canada to the Gulf of Mexico along streams, nesting in bluffs, sand or clay banks, and road cuts. Winters from New England, Ohio, and Iowa south. *Its general bluish-gray and white colors, with reddish-brown streaks on breast, large head, large bill, and loud rattling cry are very distinctive.* Catches small fishes. Might nest in sparrow-hawk size nest box.

OWLS

Owls feed mainly on small animals such as mice, rats, rabbits, and birds, generally by night, but some may catch fishes and the smaller ones eat insects. Small owls may nest in screech owl type nest houses. The cup-like formation of feathers on face is distinctive.

29. BARN OWL (*Tyto alba*). 15-21″. Resident from Iowa, Wisconsin, Ohio, and Massachusetts to the Gulf, living usually in old buildings, but sometimes in hollow trees. Forages in meadows and fields. *The white, heart-shaped face and the pale whitish or lightly reddish-brown underparts are distinctive;* generally pale brown or reddish-brown above. Has ghostly, hisslike "ksschhh!" call.

30. SCREECH OWL (*Otus asio*). 8-10″. Found mostly in woods from southern Canada to the Gulf and Florida. Two different color phases: light reddish-brown and gray. This is *the only small owl with two "horns."* Gives a down-pitched wail or tremulous whistle, not truly a screech.

31. GREAT HORNED OWL (*Bubo virginianus*). 20-24″. Resident from Hudson Bay and Labrador to Florida and the Gulf; found in many habitats, but prefers the open woods. *This is the only very large owl with two large and well-separated "horns."* It has a distinctive white throat collar, white "X" in middle of face, and reddish-brown areas on outer sides of eyes. Deep, booming three to six (often five) "hoo-hoohoo-hoo-hoo" notes.

32. SNOWY OWL (*Nyctea scandiaca*). 20-26″. Breeds in Arctic, wintering irregularly southward to Kentucky and Maryland. Flies usually by day and may be seen perched on dunes, posts, or other prominences in open areas. *The only very large, all-over white to whitish (often duskily flecked or marked) owl with a round, hornless head.*

14

29. BARN OWL

33. BARRED OWL

32. SNOWY OWL

31. GREAT HORNED OWL

34. LONG-EARED OWL

35. SHORT-EARED OWL

30. SCREECH OWL

36. SAW-WHET OWL

33. BARRED OWL *(Strix varia)*. 18-22″. Resident from southern Canada to the Gulf and Florida, frequenting swamps and wet woodlands. *The large, glowing, brown eyes and the way the bars on the breast are streaked across while the streaks on the belly extend downward are quite unique in owls.* Usually gives emphatic sharp hoots in two groups of four, with a dropping "hooo-haw" at the end. In distance often sounds like dog barking. The GREAT GRAY OWL *(Strix nebulosa)* of the far northern states and Canada is very rare but is *easily identified by color, great size (24-34″), large face discs, long tail, and round head.*

34. LONG-EARED OWL *(Asio otus)*. 13-16″. Breeds from Newfoundland and southern Canada to northern Texas, Tennessee, and Virginia, prefers evergreen forests; winters southward to the Gulf states. *This is the only middle-sized, slim owl with close-set "horns."* It has a brown back and brown-streaked breast. Call is a dove-like and moaning "hoo-hoo-hoo," also a gargled whistle and a catlike whine.

35. SHORT-EARED OWL *(Asio flammeus)*. 13-17½″. Breeds from Arctic to central tier of states; winters in southern Canada and the Great Lakes–New England area. This day-flying owl circles slowly along over open and marshy country, dropping down suddenly on a mouse or rat. *Its big round head (with only short horns), and the yellowish-brown underwing patches and black thumb-print marks at the bases of the primary feathers show distinctively in flight.* Call is a sneezelike bark.

36. SAW-WHET OWL *(Aegolius acadica)*. 7-9″. Breeds from southern Canada to West Virginia and northern Illinois; winters south to Louisiana and Virginia. *This tiny owl is hornless and streaked brown and white*, though young are dark brown with black faces and broad white "V" between eyes. Rapid bell-like "too-too-too" call.

FLYCATCHERS AND HORNED LARK

Flycatchers usually catch insects in flight by sitting on the tip of a branch, post, or other perch and periodically circling out to feed. A few warblers and other birds also do this, but not so frequently, and the flycatcher sits much more quietly on its perch. They may be attracted to suet or insect-mix hung high in trees. Accept robin-type, open nest houses.

37. WOOD PEEWEE *(Contopus virens)*. 6-6¾″. Breeds from southern Canada to Florida and Gulf States; winters in Central and South America, preferring orchards and open woods. *Its two conspicuous white wing-bars and lack of an eye-ring are distinctive;* it is dusky greenish-olive-brown above and whitish below. Unlike the phoebe, it does not wag its tail. Drawls and slurs out a plaintive "pee-a-wee"; more rarely "pee-ur."

38. OLIVE-SIDED FLYCATCHER *(Nuttalornis borealis)*. 7-8″. Breeds from southern Canada into the northern tier of states and as far south in the mountains as North Carolina; winters in South America. Inhabits brushy areas in coniferous forests. *Has two dark chest-patches separated by a white center stripe.* Gives triple-noted "pet-pet-pet" cry, and has a vigorous and cheerful song.

38. OLIVE-SIDED FLYCATCHER

37. WOOD PEEWEE

41. LEAST FLYCATCHER

42. HORNED LARK

Rh

Empidonax Flycatchers. The following three species, and the Yellow-bellied Flycatcher (discussed later), *have a white eye-ring plus yellowish-white wing bars, and an olive-brown back.* These species are whitish-bellied, and are best identified by habitat and calls as coloring is not markedly distinctive.

39. ACADIAN FLYCATCHER *(Empidonax virescens).* 5½-6½″. Found from Iowa, southern Michigan, and western New York to Florida and Gulf states, wintering in South America. *Likes beech trees, deciduous forests, and woody swamps. Has startlingly sharp "wwh-see" or "spit-see" call.* Nests in high crotches of trees.   (Not illustrated).

40. ALDER or TRAILL'S FLYCATCHER *(Empidonax traillii).* 5¼-6″. Breeds from southern Canada to Arkansas, Kentucky, mountains of West Virginia, and Connecticut; winters in Central America. *Best identified from habitation of alder swamps and streamside thickets, and by hoarse, burry, usually three-syllabled call, sounding like "wee-bea-oh" in east, but like "twitz-brew" in west; also emits low "pit" or "pet" notes.*   (Not illustrated).

41. LEAST FLYCATCHER *(Empidonax minimus).* 5-5¾″. Breeds from southern Canada to Missouri, Kentucky, mountains of North Carolina, and New Jersey; winters in Central America. *Best told by habitat of orchards, open woods, and farms, and by explosive rattling "cheh-bek!" call.* These four *Empidonax* flycatchers may mingle in migratory flights, and rarely call, so that species identification in fall and spring is often impossible. The White-eyed Vireo may be mistaken for a flycatcher, but it has a definite white spectacle instead of an eye-ring.

Other flycatchers (103-109) are discussed later.

42. HORNED LARK *(Eremophila alpestris).* 7-8″. Breeds from the Arctic to Missouri, North Carolina, and the coast of Texas; winters in Gulf states, Florida, and Georgia, preferring open areas. *The male is easily identified by two sharp black "horns," and by a distinct yellowish white bar above eye;* also by black and yellowish blotches or marks on neck and breast, contrasting with the brown body; female is duller, with less contrasting colors. Emits "tee-hee" or "tee-teetee" notes and sings a shrill, sparkling song, frequently from high in the air.

SWIFTS AND SWALLOWS

43. CHIMNEY SWIFT *(Chaetura pelagica).* 5-5½″. Breeds from New-foundland and southern Canada to the Gulf, nesting in chimneys. *Though it looks like a brownish-black swallow, it belongs to an entirely different family, and differs by having a much shorter tail, and even longer, thinner wings that appear to twinkle alternately in flight somewhat like those of a bat,* followed by short glides during which wings are positioned in crescent-shape. Notes have machine-gun-like ticking or chippering sound. Catches insects while in fast flight.

Swallows are sparrow-size birds with long narrow wings; their graceful flight is made with even wing-beats followed by long glides; the average-length tails are usually notched or v-shaped. They feed on insects while in regular flight patterns.

43. CHIMNEY SWIFT

44. TREE SWALLOW

46. ROUGH-WINGED SWALLOW

45. BANK SWALLOW

47. BARN SWALLOW

48. CLIFF SWALLOW

♂

♀

Rh

49. PURPLE MARTIN

44. TREE SWALLOW *(Iridoprocne bicolor)*. 5-6". Breeds from southern Canada to Virginia, Tennessee, and Arkansas; winters from North Carolina to Florida and Gulf states. Usually found near water and woods, especially in swamps. *Distinguished from other swallows by sharply contrasting white underparts and dark upperparts (bluish or black-green in adults, brown in juvenile birds).* May be lured to blue-bird size houses placed on posts in open. Has "cheep" or "cheet" or "chee-veet" notes, and a gurgling, liquid song.

45. BANK SWALLOW *(Riparia riparia)*. 5-5½". Breeds from southern Canada to northern areas of the Gulf states and to Virginia on the coast; winters in South America. Nests in sand banks and road-cuts. Has distinctively brown back combined with dark brown band across the chest. Nests in holes in clay banks. Gives a quick, dry, and rattling series of buzzy notes, like "breet!" or "bzzt!"

46. ROUGH-WINGED SWALLOW *(Stelgidopteryx ruficollis)*. 5-6". Breeds from southeast Ontario and northern tier of states to the Gulf; winters in Central America; nests in stream banks or near water in crevices in walls and other structures. *The lighter brown of the back, the bright white of the belly merging into a dingy, light brown on the breast and throat, and the distinct breast band distinguish this bird from other brown-backed swallows.* Similar voice to that of preceding bird, but more ragged or rough sounding.

47. BARN SWALLOW *(Hirundo rustica)*. 6-7½". Breeds from southern Canada south, sometimes as far as the Gulf Coast. Winters from Mexico to South America. Constructs open nests of mud, usually in barns and other buildings; prefers open areas. *The deeply-forked tail with two white spots at base is conspicuously distinctive;* has blue-black back, dark reddish-brown throat, set off by dark line from the light reddish-brown or pinkish breast and belly, which is white in the rear portion. Call a soft "kvit" or "kvik-vik."

48. CLIFF SWALLOW *(Petrochelidon pyrrhonota)*. 5-6". Breeds from southern Canada to western Virginia, northern Alabama, and Louisiana. Builds closed, ball-shaped nests under bridges, on cliffs, and on outer surfaces of buildings, particularly barns. *Has distinctive square-ending tail, bright orange-brown or reddish-brown rump, and a dark reddish-brown throat patch.* Gives a rough-edged, squeaky "vik-vik" call.

49. PURPLE MARTIN *(Progne subis)*. 7½-8½". Breeds from southern Canada to the Gulf States. Often uses blue-bird size houses or gourds with 2½" wide entrance holes, if hung out on wire in multiples in open area for colony; also nests in other man-made structures. *Large size, plus the overall glossy blue-black color make the male very distinctive;* the female is more brownish-black on back with grayish-brown breast and throat collar. A deep, husky "chew-hew" or "tchu-wu" is its call.

CHICKADEES, TITMOUSE, AND WRENS

Chickadees and Titmice are extremely active small birds, flitting about the smaller branches and twigs of trees, *often upside-down*, searching for small insects. They have rather long tails, and small, short bills. They may be attracted to suet or insect-mix, and will occupy wren-sized houses, especially if well-hidden.

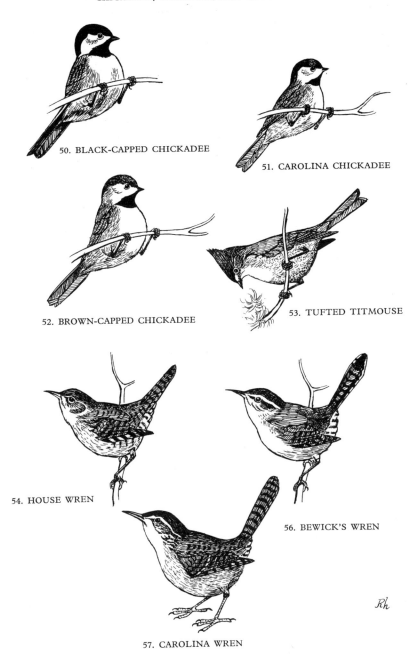

50. BLACK-CAPPED CHICKADEE

51. CAROLINA CHICKADEE

52. BROWN-CAPPED CHICKADEE

53. TUFTED TITMOUSE

54. HOUSE WREN

56. BEWICK'S WREN

57. CAROLINA WREN

Rh

50. BLACK-CAPPED CHICKADEE *(Parus atricapillus)*. 4¾-5½". Resident from Newfoundland and southern Canada to New Jersey, Ohio, and Missouri, also in North Carolina mountains. A black bib and black cap contrasting with the white cheeks and breast are characteristic of most chickadees. *The larger size, whitish area on wing, and larger area of pink suffusion on the belly distinguish this species from the very similar Carolina Chickadee.* Has a sharply-spoken "chick-a-dee-dee-dee" or "dee-dee" call, and a brightly whistled "see-bee" or "fee-bee-dee."

51. CAROLINA CHICKADEE *(Parus carolinensis)*. 4¼-4¾". Resident from Missouri, Ohio, and New Jersey (generally south of the Black-capped Chickadee's range) and to the Gulf and Florida. Except for smaller size, this bird very closely resembles the Black-capped species. It has more quickly repeated and shriller voice, however, and prefers a more southern habitat.

52. BROWN-CAPPED CHICKADEE *(Parus hudsonicus)*. 5-5½". Resident from limit of trees in Canada, mainly in spruce forests, to mountains of Minnesota, Michigan, New York, and northern New England; also wintering sometimes into New Jersey and Pennsylvania. *Identified by brown cap and back;* those of other chickadees are grayer. Lazy notes of "sick-adeeeeeee;" wheezy "chik-chee-day-day."

53. TUFTED TITMOUSE *(Parus bicolor)*. 6-6½". Resident in Iowa, Indiana, and New Jersey to Florida and Gulf states. Common in orchards and open woods. *Has very distinctive tufted crest and overall soft gray color.* Has nasal and wheezy chickadee-like notes and also whistled "here-here-here" or "peter-peter-peter."

Wrens are small, thick-bodied, comparatively long and sharp-billed, brown birds frequenting bushes and tangles; often cock tails over their backs, and usually scold noisily when an intruder gets near. Will usually nest in wrenhouses; all eat insect mix, suet, and table scraps.

54. HOUSE WREN *(Troglodytes aedon)*. 4½-4¼". Breeds from southern Canada to Missouri, Kentucky, and Virginia; winters just south of this area to Gulf states. *Over-all gray-brown color without facial stripings is distinctive.* Has a scolding voice, and a stuttering, liquid gurgling song.

55. WINTER WREN *(Troglodytes troglodytes)*. (Not illustrated). Very similar in range and appearance to the house wren but has a *much shorter tail and white and brown-barred belly.* Note is a sharp "kip-kip."

56. BEWICK'S WREN *(Thryomanes bewickii)*. 5-5½". Found from Iowa, southern Michigan, Indiana, and New Jersey to northern parts of South Carolina and Gulf states. *Easily recognized by white spots on long tail and the white stripe over the eye.* Two or three high notes start song, which ends in weak trill.

57. CAROLINA WREN *(Thryothorus ludovicianus)*. 5½-6". Resident from southern Iowa, Ohio, Pennsylvania, and Rhode Island to the Gulf states and Florida. *The reddish-brown wings and tail and white wing bars are distinctive;* otherwise dark brown above and light brown and whitish below. Very clear chanting whistle in groups of two to three syllables.

MOCKINGBIRD, CATBIRD, THRASHER, GNATCATCHER, BLACKBIRDS, AND PIPIT

The first four birds discussed may be attracted to robin-type, open nest, bird boxes.

58. MOCKINGBIRD *(Mimus polyglottos)*. 9-11″. Resident in towns and farms from southern Iowa, Illinois, Ohio, and Maryland to the Gulf; a rare few farther north in summer. Same size as a Robin, but longer-tailed and more slender *with gray back and white belly; large white patches show in wings and tail in flight.* Mockingbirds are noted mimics of other birds in their songs, but can usually be recognized by the way they rapidly repeat each musical phrase, often six times or more. Has loud "tchak" note. Feeds on insects, seeds, and berries.

59. CATBIRD *(Dumetella carolinensis)*. 8½-9¼″. Breeds, preferably in dense bushes, from southern Canada to Gulf states and northern Florida. *The slaty-gray back, black cap, and bright reddish-brown under tail base are distinctive.* Mews very much like a cat. Song very jumbled and only partly musical. Eats insects and fleshy fruits.

60. BROWN THRASHER *(Toxostoma rufum)*. 10½-12″. Breeds from southern Canada to Gulf states and northern Florida; winters in southern states, preferring brushy areas and thickets. *Reddish-brown color above, two white bars, dark brown-streaked breast, long tail, and comparatively long, strong bill are distinctive.* Sings deliberately in succession of paired phrases; hoarse "tchak" note. Eats insects, lizards, amphibians, berries, acorns, and seeds.

61. BLUE-GRAY GNATCATCHER *(Polioptila caerulea)*. 4½-5″. Breeds from southern border of Ontario, in Iowa, Ohio, and Pennsylvania to Gulf states and Florida. Frequents woods. *Distinctive long black tail with white edges, white spectacle around eye, bluish-gray back, and white undersurfaces.* Very thin, querulous "pzzeee" note. Eats insects.

62. WATER PIPIT *(Anthus spinoletta)*. 6-7″. Breeds in the Arctic; winters in open areas from New Jersey and southern Illinois to the Gulf states and northern Florida. *Distinctive constant wagging of tail, slender bill, dark brown streaks on yellow-brown underparts, and white outer tail feathers identify it.* A thin "pee-eeet" cry is frequently heard as bird flies overhead. Feeds on insects, seeds of spurge and other weeds.

63. RUSTY BLACKBIRD *(Euphagus carolinus)*. 8-9¼″. Breeds from Canada to northern Minnesota, Michigan, New York, and New England; winters mainly in southern United States in wet woodlands and swamps. *In spring and summer the male is all black with a yellowish white eye; female is more grayish with white eye; both become suffused with rusty color in fall.* Feeds on insects, grain, and weed seeds. Gives a loud "chuk" note and has song like the creaking of a rusty hinge.

64. BREWER'S BLACKBIRD *(Euphagus cyanocephalus.* (Not illustrated.) Found in prairies of Minnesota, Wisconsin, and northern Illinois. Similar to the rusty blackbird, but male has more purplish reflections and iridescence; female has dark eye. Similar call, song, and food.

MOCKINGBIRD, CATBIRD, THRASHER, GNATCATCHER, BLACKBIRDS, AND PIPIT

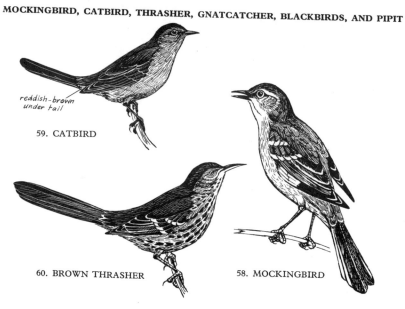

reddish-brown
under tail

59. CATBIRD

60. BROWN THRASHER

58. MOCKINGBIRD

61. BLUE-GRAY GNATCATCHER

63. RUSTY BLACKBIRD

62. WATER PIPIT

65. COMMON GRACKLE

Rh

65. COMMON GRACKLE *(Quisculus quiscula)*. 11-13″. Breeds from southern Canada to Florida and the Gulf. *The long wedge or keel-shaped tail is characteristic, as is the very long powerful bill, and the iridescent purplish, bronze or green colors on the black back.* The females are generally brownish. Eats insects, worms, amphibians, mice, corn and other grains, and weed seeds. Call note is a sharp "chek!" Has a trilling summer song, rising and dropping in pitch.

SPARROWS

Sparrows have rather short, thick bills, useful in eating seeds, which form their main diet, but insects are eaten also. Some may nest in robin-type, open, bird houses.

Sparrows first discussed have at least some streaking on the breast.

66. VESPER SPARROW *(Pooecetes gramineus)*. 5½-6½″. Breeds in open areas from southern Canada south to Missouri, Kentucky, and North Carolina. Winters from southern edge of breeding range to Gulf states and Florida. *Unlike similar Song Sparrow, has whitish eye-ring and no central spot on chest; white outer tail feathers flash in flight; also shows reddish-brown patch at bend of wing.* Begins song with two clear whistles followed by two more at higher pitch.

67. SONG SPARROW *(Melospiza melodia)*. 5-7″. Breeds from Canada to Missouri, Illinois, coastal North Carolina, and mountains of Georgia. Winters from Iowa, southern Ontario, and Massachusetts to Gulf and Florida. *Breast heavily streaked with brown, coming together in large central spot; tail is pumped up and down in flight.* Young birds have finer streaks and sometimes no spot. The repeated, familiar song is of three or four "seet-sweet-sweet" notes.

68. LINCOLN'S SPARROW *(Melospiza lincolni)*. 5¼-6″. Breeds from Newfoundland and forested areas of Canada to northern Minnesota, Michigan, New York, and Maine, usually in swamps and damp meadows. Winters along southeast Atlantic coast and in Gulf states. *Similar to the song sparrow, but has finer, dark brown streaking on breast and a broad, creamy-brown band across the breast.* Sweet, gurgling, up-lilting song.

69. SAVANNAH SPARROW *(Passerculus sandwichensis)*. 5¼-6″. Breeds in meadows and prairies from Canada to Long Island, New Jersey, Pennsylvania, and northern Illinois and Iowa. Winters from south edge of breeding range to Florida and Gulf. Similar in appearance to Lincoln's and Savannah sparrows but has shorter, *notched tail, a yellow stripe over the eye, and a white stripe through middle of head.* Song a sleepy, lisping "tsi-tsi-tsi, tseeeeee-tsaaaay," with low-pitched final note.

70. FOX SPARROW *(Passerella iliaca)*. 6½-7½″. Breeds mainly in spruce forests from tree-limit in Canada to northern Manitoba and Gulf of St. Lawrence; winters in woods and brushy tangles from Ohio Valley and Massachusetts to Florida and Gulf states. *The large size for a sparrow, bright reddish-brown tail and heavy reddish-brown streaks on breast are distinctive.* Often vigorously scratches at leaf-litter under bushes.

71. HENSLOW'S SPARROW *(Passerherbulus henslowii)*. 4½-5¼″. Breeds from southern Minnesota, Wisconsin, Michigan, and New Hampshire to Missouri, West Virginia, and northern North Carolina, usually in weedy meadows. *The sharp tail, reddish-brown wings, dark stripes on olive-brown head, and gray neck-band are distinctive.* Unmusical, hiccuping "ts-lik" song.

72. SHARP-TAILED SPARROW *(Amnospiza caudacuta)*. 5-6″. Breeds in salt marshes from Gulf of St. Lawrence and St. Lawrence River along Atlantic Coast to Virginia and inland in Minnesota prairie marshes; winters along Atlantic and Gulf coasts and in Florida. Many varieties, but all have *orange-yellow on face, surrounding a gray ear patch;* those on coast have breasts streaked, but inland form has less or no streaking. Song a hissing, husky, gasping buzz like "tut-tut-szeeeeee." Compare with 81.

SPARROWS WITH STREAKED BREASTS

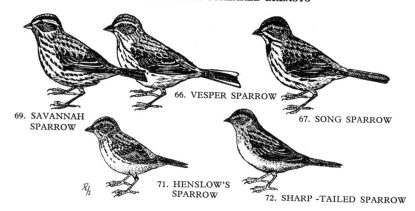

69. SAVANNAH SPARROW

66. VESPER SPARROW

67. SONG SPARROW

71. HENSLOW'S SPARROW

72. SHARP -TAILED SPARROW

SPARROWS

Most sparrows discussed here have unstreaked breasts.

73. HOUSE or ENGLISH SPARROW *(Passer domesticus)*. (Does not belong to family containing the other sparrows, nor does 74, but put here because of similar appearance). 5-6¼″. Resident in farms, towns, and cities almost everywhere; individuals in towns get colors obscured by dust and soot. *The black throat, gray crown, reddish-brown and black striped back, white wing bars are distinctive in male;* female more general brown-grey above and dull whitish below. Constant quarrelsome notes.

74. EUROPEAN TREE SPARROW *(Passer montanus)*. (Not illustrated.) Same size; resident in St. Louis area. Both sexes similar to male of preceding species except for chocolate crown and large black spot back of eye. A hoarse "tek-tek" call.

73. HOUSE or ENGLISH SPARROW

75. LARK SPARROW

76. PINE WOODS SPARROW

77. FIELD SPARROW

79. CHIPPING SPARROW

80. TREE SPARROW

75. LARK SPARROW *(Chondestes grammacus)*. 5½-6½". Breeds from southern Manitoba and Ontario southward through Mississippi Valley to northern Louisiana and northeast to West Virginia; winters in Gulf states west of Florida. *The fan-shaped black tail with white outside corners, the reddish-brown, white, and black stripes, and blotches on head and face are very distinctive, as is the single black spot on the clear breast.* Song broken up among clear whistles, trills, and churring and buzzing notes.

76. PINE WOODS SPARROW *(Aimophila aestivalis)*. 5½-6". Breeds from southeast Iowa, central Illinois, Indiana, southern Ohio, southwest Pennsylvania, and Maryland, south to Florida and the Gulf Coast in open pine woods. Winters from North Carolina south. Very shy, hiding in brush, but reveals glimpses of its *clear yellowish-brown to whitish breast and its brown and reddish-brown streaked back.* Song a bright liquid whistle, turning into a differently pitched broken trill or warble, "seee-sip-sip, etc."

77. FIELD SPARROW *(Spizella pusilla)*. 5¼-6". Breeds from southern Minnesota, Ontario, southern Quebec, and southern Maine south to northern edge of Gulf states and Floirda, in brushy fields and clearings. *Pink bill and markedly reddish-brown colors on back, head, and wings are distinctive.* Gives questioning "tzeee" note; song a series of clear and slurred notes.

78. CLAY-COLORED SPARROW *(Spizella pallida)*. (Not illustrated.) 5-5½". Breeds in central Canada, and south to northern Iowa, Illinois, and north central Michigan, frequenting brushy prairies, pine barrens, and woodlands. *Looks something like Field and Chipping Sparrows, but sharply marked brown ear-patch, and whitish stripe through the crown are different;* the immature bird is distinguished by its yellowish-brown rump. Very distinctive un-bird-like song of three or four soft buzzes.

79. CHIPPING SPARROW *(Spizella passerina)*. 5-5½". Breeds from southern Canada southward into northern edge of Gulf states; winters mainly in southern states, but sometimes as/far north as New Jersey and Ohio Valley. *The bright reddish-brown cap, black line through eye, and white line over eye are distinctive;* brownish above. The song is a single-pitched, dry rattle or trill of "tsip" sounds.

80. TREE SPARROW *(Spizella arborea)*. 6-6½". Breeds in far northern Canada, but comes south in winter as far as Arkansas and South Carolina. *Instantly recognized by bright red-brown cap and a large round black spot in center of breast.* Has a sharp "tseeet" note, and also a musical "leeler" or "leelvit" call.

SPARROWS, JUNCOS, AND BUNTINGS

81. LE CONTE'S SPARROW *(Passerherbulus caudacutus)*. (Compare with 71 to 72.) Breeds in prairie marshes from north central Canada to Minnesota; winters south and east to Gulf states, South Carolina, and Florida. *Identified by the sharp tail ends, bright yellow-brown stripe above eye, and the wide brownish-pink collar on the neck of the adult;* also has a white stripe through the crown and is *streaked only on side of breast.* The thin barely audible song is made up of two light hisses, the second stronger.

68. LINCOLN'S SPARROW

70. FOX SPARROW

84. WHITE-CROWNED SPARROW

83. WHITE-THROATED SPARROW

82. GRASSHOPPER SPARROW

85. HARRIS'S SPARROW

81. LE CONTE'S SPARROW

86. SLATE-COLORED JUNCO

87. SNOW BUNTING

82. **GRASSHOPPER SPARROW** *(Ammodramus savannarum).* 5-5½″. Breeds in prairies and meadows from southern Minnesota, Michigan, Ontario, and New Hampshire south to Gulf states and central Florida. Winters from southern Illinois and North Carolina south. *The short tail, flat head, unstreaked yellowish-brown breast, and heavily striped back are distinctive.* It has two songs, the first long, tumbling in tone like the buzz of a groggy bumble-bee, the second with two soft notes followed by a weak slightly rattling buzz, or something like "tip-tip, zeeeeeeeeeeeeeeeee."

83. **WHITE-THROATED SPARROW** *(Zonotrichia albicollis).* 6½-7¼″. Breeds from Newfoundland and southern Canada to Minnesota, New England, and in mountains to northeast Pennsylvania; winters from Massachusetts and Ohio Valley south to Gulf. Usually found in brushy edges of forest and dense brush. White crown and eyestripe make it look like the White-crowned Sparrow, but *the sharp, white throat patch contrasting with gray breast is very unique among sparrows.* Starts song with two clear, plaintive, whistling notes, then three quivering notes on different pitch. Has sharp "kink" note, or fuzzy "tsleet."

84. **WHITE-CROWNED SPARROW** *(Zonotrichia leucophrys).* 6½-7½″. Breeds in northern Canada; often migrant into Mississippi Valley; usually winters west of Appalachian Mountains from the Ohio Valley to Gulf. *White and black striped head appears quite high; grayish throat and breast;* juvenile with brown and yellowish-brown head stripes. Song starts plaintively as that of the preceding species, but is with a rough trill.

85. **HARRIS'S SPARROW** *(Zonotrichia querula.)* 7-7¾″. Breeds among low bushes and stunted spruces at northern edge of tree zone west of Hudson's Bay; migrates through Illinois, southwest Ohio, and Michigan to winter in Missouri and Arkansas. Frequents brush and weed patches. *Large size, high, black-brown and black face, throat, and breast, and pink bill are very distinctive,* but adults in winter may appear more grayish on head, while juveniles have white on throat and yellowish-brown on head. Often appears to chuckle as it gives hints of delicate, quivering song in winter.

86. **SLATE-COLORED JUNCO** *(Junco hyemalis).* 6-6½″. Breeds in coniferous forests of Canada to northern tier of states and down Appalachians to northern Georgia; winters from southern Canada to the Gulf. *The contrasting white of the belly and outer tail feathers against the slate-gray general color is distinctive.* Utters soft, clicking, smacking, and twittering notes; song a shaky trill.

87. **SNOW BUNTING** *(Plectrophenax nivalis).* 6-7¼″. Breeds in Arctic; winters southward to northern United States and down Atlantic Coast to North Carolina. *The over-all white color is distinctive,* but there is reddish-brown on head and shoulders and brown and brownish-black markings on back, wings, and tail; *large white wing patches flash in flight.* Very clear, whistled "teew" or "teer" notes; also purrs musically and has hoarse "bzzzt" call.

DOVES

89. ROCK DOVE or DOMESTIC PIGEON 88. MOURNING DOVE

90. GROUND DOVE

DOVES

88. MOURNING DOVE *(Zenaidura macroura)*. 11-13″. Breeds from southern Canada to the Gulf; winters from Iowa, Michigan, and Massachusetts south. Frequents weedlands, grasslands, brush, farms, and gardens. Smaller and slimmer than the Domestic Pigeon or Rock Dove, with a *very long, pointed tail, pink with large white spots showing in flight,* pink-gray belly and breast, yellowish-brown head, and black spot just behind and below eye. In flight the wings produce a whistling sound. Has a mournful "ooh, coo-coo-coo" call. Seeds of bristlegrass, corn, wheat, and miscellaneous weed seeds are favorite foods. May be induced to nest in robin-type nest in low trees or large bushes.

89. ROCK DOVE or DOMESTIC PIGEON *(Columba livia)*. 15-16″. Lives in or near farms, towns, and cities. *Head, neck, and body purplish gray, somewhat irridescent.* Soft cooing call. Will nest in large bird house such as for Sparrow Hawk, but prefers colony of several houses. Feeds mainly on grains.

90. GROUND DOVE *(Columbigallina passerina)*. 6½-7″. Resident of lowlands and coastal plains from South Carolina through Gulf states. *A sparrow-sized dove with blackish tail having white spot at corners, blackish back and first part of wings, but reddish-brown on primary feathers, flashing in flight.* Red color disappears when wings are folded and this may fool pursuing enemy. Nods head when walking. Voice is a moaning "ooo-oo, wooo-oo, wooo-oo" repeated over and over. Feeds on seeds of dove weed and paspalum, as well as on those of various grasses and weeds.

31

WOODPECKERS

Woodpeckers have powerful bills for drilling into wood or bark, usually for insect grubs; all have two toes projecting forward and two backward. The stiff, almost spine-like tails prop up bodies when positioned on tree trunks. Flight pattern is vertically undulating. Some will nest in large, stump-shaped bird houses. Feeds mainly on insects, particularly grubs under bark.

91. YELLOW-SHAFTED FLICKER *(Colaptes auratus)*. 13-14″ long. Breeds from tree limit in Canada to the Gulf states and Florida; winters from Great Lakes region and New England south. Habituates open woods. *The white rump contrasting sharply with the brown back, and the flash of yellow under the wings and tail as the bird flies are conspicuous;* also has red patch at top of neck. Very loud "wick-wick-wick-wick" call, rapidly repeated; a "kee-er" note and wheezy "flick, flicka" series. Eats ants, beetles and other insects, and berries of various bushes and poison ivy.

92. PILEATED WOODPECKER *(Hylatomus pileatus)*. 17-20″. Habitat, primarily in coniferous forests, but also in other dense woods, from southern Canada to the Gulf states and Florida. *The large size and the conspicuous brilliant red crest and the flash of black and white colors in flight are distinctive.* The very large oblong or oval holes it digs in tree trunks are sure marks of its presence. Has very loud stuttering "huk—huk—huk-huk-huk—huk-huk" call. It has another call more ringing and undulating in pitch. Feeds on ants, beetles, grubs, and the fruits of wild grapes, blackgum, and various bushes.

93. RED-BELLIED WOODPECKER *(Centurus carolinus)*. 9-10¾″. Habitat is from southeast Minnesota, Ohio, southern Ontario, and Delaware to the Gulf states and Florida. Frequents broad-leaf tree forests, and large trees near dwellings. *This is the only woodpecker with a complete red cap in male, combined with a yellow and black barred back;* female has red on top of neck, brownish on head while immature, but zebra-backed. A churring, chawing, chivying call; also a subdued "flicka-flicka-flicka" series of notes. Beetles, ants, and other insects are eaten, but it also feeds on acorns, wild grapes, corn, and wild berries.

94. RED-HEADED WOODPECKER *(Melanerpes erythrocephalus)*. 8½-9½″. Breeds from southern Manitoba, Minnesota, southern Ontario, western New York, and southern New England south to Gulf states. Prefers open woods and prairies with scattered trees. *This is the only woodpecker of our region with a completely red head. The large white patches on the outer parts of the wings show conspicuously in flight;* immature birds have these patches, but head is blackish-brown. Gives loud "kerrr" or "kreeeoh" call, shriller than that of Red-bellied Woodpecker. Feeds on such as beetles, ants, bees, acorns, corn, and cherries.

95. YELLOW-BELLIED SAPSUCKER *(Sphyrapicus varius)*. 8-8½″. Breeds from southern Canada to Missouri, Indiana, Pennsylvania, Delaware, and down mountains to North Carolina; winters from Wisconsin, southern Michigan, and southern New England to Gulf states and Florida. Frequents mixed broad-leaf and coniferous woods. *A long, white patch contrasting sharply with the black on wing, and the red patch on forehead are distinctive; male has red throat.* Has squealing, slurred "mew" call, somewhat like that of a cat or jay; drums on trees in rhythm of rapid thumps followed immediately by slow ones. Feeds on sap from trees and also eats various insects.

WOODPECKERS AND HUMMINGBIRDS

96. HAIRY WOODPECKER *(Dendrocopus villosus)*. 8½-10½″. Resident from southern Canada to Gulf states and Florida in both coniferous and broad-leaved woods. This, along with the Downy, is a white-backed woodpecker. They are similar in appearance, with black and white design in both sexes, and red patch on back of head in the male, but this species is much larger with far more powerful bill. Makes loud drumming noise on trees. Has loud "keek!" note and rattling call. Diet includes beetle grubs, ants, and other insects supplemented with fruits of poison ivy, dogwood, and various bushes.

97. DOWNY WOODPECKER *(Dendrocopus pubescens)*. 6¼-7″. Resident from southern Canada to Gulf states and Florida in more open woods than above bird, and is more often found in shade trees around homes, parks, and orchards. Often keeps company with chickadees, nuthatches, and titmice. Looks like small twin of above woodpecker, but *has black bars along white edge of tail*. The whinny-like notes descend in pitch at the end, and are not so rapidly repeated as to sound like the rattle of the Hairy Woodpecker. The bill hammered on trees makes a light tattooing sound. Eats particularly wood-boring beetle grubs and boring moth larvae but also feeds on other insects and spiders, and the berries of poison-ivy, dogwood, and various bushes.

98. RED-COCKADED WOODPECKER *(Dendrocopus borealis)*. Resident mainly in open pine woods of southern states, rarely coming north as far as Virginia, Kentucky, and southern Missouri. *The black neck and top of head, combined with the bright white cheeks, and black and cream, barred back are distinctive;* the red spot on the side of the head is not always easy to see. Has rough, file-like "zripppp" or "zwilkp" notes; also a high, thin "sick" call. Feeds on various insects, pine nuts, corn, acorns, and berries.

99. ARCTIC THREE-TOED, or BLACK-BACKED WOODPECKER *(Picoides arcticus)*. (Not illustrated). 9-10″. Found in deep spruce forests of southern Canada and the northernmost states. *The solid black back, yellow crown, and black bars on white sides are distinctive.*

100. AMERICAN THREE-TOED WOODPECKER *(Picoides tridactylus)*. 8-9½″. Similar habitat and appearance of preceding species, but *has white and black-barred, ladder-patterned back. Both these woodpeckers are the only ones with yellow cap on head and three toes on feet.* They feed mainly on wood-boring grubs and larvae.

Hummingbirds are *easily recognized by tiny size, long thin bills, and buzzing, hovering flight.* Feed on tiny insects and nectar, and may be lured to humming-bird feeders.

101. RUBY-THROATED HUMMINGBIRD *(Archilochus colubris)*. 3-3¾″. Breeds from southern Canada to the Gulf states and Florida; winters from Florida south. Often seen in flower gardens and parks. Colored mettalic-green above; *the male flashes a bright red throat; female has white throat.* During mating season, the male often emits buzzing sounds while making arcing dives at the female.

102. RUFOUS HUMMINGBIRD *(Selasphorus rufus)*. (Not illustrated). 3¼-3½″. Rare winter visitor along Gulf coast from Louisiana to northern Florida. *The only hummingbird in our region with bright reddish-brown back and tail;* male has flaming red throat.

WOODPECKERS

93. RED-BELLIED WOODPE

immature

91. YELLOW-SHAFTED FLICKER

immature

RED-HEAD

94. RED-HEADED
WOODPECKER

92. PILEATED WOODPECKER

Rosinda Holmes

95. YELLOW-BELLIED
SAPSUCKER

immature

98. RED-COCKADED
WOODPECKER

96. HAIRY
WOODPECKER

97. DOWNY WOODPECKER

KINGBIRDS, FLYCATCHERS, AND JAY
(See also other flycatchers, 37–41)

103. **EASTERN KINGBIRD** *(Tyrannus tyrannus)*. 8¼-9″. Breeds from southern Canada south to Gulf states and Florida; winters in tropics. Inhabits open areas. *Instantly told by nearly all-black color above, contrasting with wide, white band on end of tail and white underparts; red crest* on top of head rarely seen. Has sputtering, scolding, nervous notes; and a file-like nasal "bzeeb" call. Often attacks other birds.

104. **GRAY KINGBIRD** *(Tyrannus dominicensis)*. 9-9½″. Breeds in scattered localities along both coasts of Florida and sparingly in South Carolina, preferably in mangrove swamps. Resembles Eastern Kingbird, but is larger and *has light gray* instead of black on back, blackish, well-notched tail without white band, and is whitish below. Wavy "pity-cheerry" call.

105. **SCISSOR-TAILED FLYCATCHER** *(Muscivora forficata)*. (Not illustrated). 11-15″. Occasional visitor along western borders of Missouri, Arkansas, and Louisiana. *Instantly recognized by enormously long and forked tail with black tips; red marks at base of wings and top of head, and reddish suffusions on gray sides.*

106. **CRESTED FLYCATCHER** *(Myiarchus crinitus)*. 8-9″. Breeds from southern Canada to Gulf states and Florida; winters in southern Florida and tropics. Inhabits open woodlands. *The only flycatcher with a reddish-brown tail.* Whistles loudly, with rising "sweeeeeeep" inflection; also has hoarse, rolling "trrrrreeeet" call.

107. **EASTERN PHOEBE** *(Sayornis phoebe)*. 6½-7″. Breeds from southern Canada to Florida and Gulf states; winters in southern states. *Noted for constant wagging of tail and general gray-brown color* (with only dull wing bars and no eye ring); whitish below. Has "fee-bee" or "fee-bree" note.

108. **YELLOW-BELLIED FLYCATCHER** *(Empidonax flaviventris)*. (See also 39 to 41). 5-5½″. Breeds from southern Canada southward into northern tier of states, generally in wet coniferous forests and meadows; migrates throughout the east and south to Central America. *The only small flycatcher with a bright all-yellowish belly,* otherwise olive-brown with yellowish-white wing bars and eye-ring. Has a very weak simple "pur-wee" or "chur-wee" call.

109. **VERMILION FLYCATCHER** *(Pyrocephalus rubinus)*. 5½-6½″. Occasional winter visitor along Gulf Coast from western Florida to Texas. *The brilliantly contrasting black and flaming red colors of male are highly distinctive.* Female is brown above, with pinkish to orange sides, streaked with brown; young female has yellowish belly. Twitters with "zee-treee" or "pi-pi-pit-seeee" calls.

Jays feed on insects, seeds, fruits, small animals, and birds; they may be attracted by bird seed, suet, insect mix, and table scraps. May use Robin-type open bird boxes.

110. **CANADA JAY** *(Perisoreus canadensis)*. 11-13″. Inhabits spruce forests from tree limit in Canada to northern border of the United States. *The white on top of head, black on rear of head, and black strip through eye, combined with white*

throat, cheeks, collar, and gray back and wings are very distinctive. Young birds are darker, especially around head. Has many notes, both soft and harsh.

Other flycatchers were previously discussed; see 37 to 41.

JAYS, RAVEN, CROW, WAXWINGS, AND SHRIKES

111. BLUE JAY *(Cyanocitta cristata)*. 11-12″. Habitat woods, gardens, and brushy tangles from southern Canada to the Gulf states and Florida. *The bright contrasting blue, white, gray, and black colors of this large-crested jay are distinctive.* It is characteristically cocky and aggressive. Has many notes, both harsh and musical, the most common is a rough slurred "chay" or "cheeah," sometimes rapidly repeated; may scream like a hawk.

112. SCRUB or FLORIDA JAY *(Aphelocoma coerulescens)*. 11-12″. Resident in the scrub oak woods of Florida. The only jay in Florida without a crest. *Distinctive blue and light brown colors above, with blackish bars on face and whitish below.* A friendly bird, often coming to offered food of many kinds. The harsh, rasping call of "chweah-chweah" or "chwesh" is not repeated as often or as rapidly as that of the Blue Jay. Has also a shriek-like "zwreek," and a rather pleasing song of sweet tones, both high and low in pitch, mixed together and slurred or trilled.

113. RAVEN *(Corvus corax)*. (Not illustrated). 21-27″. Inhabits wild areas from northern Canada to the northern states and through the mountains to northern Georgia. *Easily recognized as one of our two very large, completely black birds, and the one that soars with horizontal wings.*

114. CROW *(Corvus brachyrhnchos)*. 17-21″. (Not illustrated). This other *large, even-toned, black bird,* usually flies in flocks, and *soars like a Turkey vulture with wings held up at an angle.* Resident all over our region.

115. CEDAR WAXWING *(Bombycilla cedrorum)*. 6½-8″. Breeds from southern Canada to Missouri, Tennessee, and northern Georgia; winters generally in central and southern tiers of states. Prefers bushy areas and open woods where it feeds on fruits and berries, particularly of red cedars, wild cherries, and dogwood. It also eats beetles, ants, and other insects. *A sleek-looking, crested, brown bird with a black mask, red spot on wing, and yellow band at end of tail.* May be attracted to robin-type open nest box. Has lisping "seee" and "zeeee" notes.

116. BOHEMIAN WAXWING *(Bombycilla garrulus)*. 7-8″. (Not illustrated). Breeds in western Canada, but occasionally winters in Minnesota, Iowa, Wisconsin, and northeastern states. Very similar to the Cedar Waxwing, but has more of *white blotches and streaks on wings, and some reddish-pink color around face.* Has rough, strong "zrrreee" note.

117. LOGGERHEAD SHRIKE *(Lanius ludovicianus)*. 8½-9½″. Breeds from southern Canada to Gulf states and Florida. Winters from Iowa, Ohio, New York, and southern New England south, generally seen in open country, orchards, or meadows, occupying a conspicuous perch to watch for its prey. Wings appear to flicker as it flies. *The large head, hooked beak, slim tail, conspicuous black mask, and general gray and white colors are distinctive.* Song is of

HUMMINGBIRD, KINGBIRD, AND FLYCATCHERS

♀ 101. RUBY-THROATED HUMMINGBIRD

♂

106. CRESTED FLYCATCHER

103. EASTERN KINGBIRD

104. GRAY KINGBIRD

107. EASTERN PHOEBE

108. YELLOW-BELLIED FLYCATCHER

109. VERMILION FLYCATCHER

Rosinda Holmes

110. CANADA JAY

111. BLUE JAY

112. SCRUB or
FLORIDA JAY

115. CEDAR WAXWING

118. NORTHERN SHRIKE

117. LOGGERHEAD SHRIK

rather weak notes and phrases repeated over and over, but is slower and more deliberate than that of the Mockingbird. Eats large insects, mice, lizards, and small birds, often impaling prey on thorn or barb of wire fence. May nest in open robin-type nest house.

118. NORTHERN SHRIKE *(Lanius excubitor)*. 9-10½". Breeds from tree limit in Canada to southern Canada; winters south as far as Missouri and Virginia. Similar to the Loggerhead Shrike but has fine barring on breast. Young birds are brownish.

NUTHATCHES, CREEPER, KINGLETS, AND THRUSHES

Nuthatches are noted for long, sharp bills, stubby tails, and habit of going down tree trunks head-first. Feed on insects, spiders, pine nuts, and acorns.

119. WHITE-BREASTED NUTHATCH *(Sitta carolinensis)*. 5-6". Frequents woods from southern Canada to Florida and the Gulf states. Black cap and black eye surrounded by white area are distinctive. Has "yank-yank" or "zank" call. May nest in blue-bird type nest box hidden in tree branches. Song of low nasal whistles.

120. RED-BREASTED NUTHATCH *(Sitta canadensis)*. 4½-5". Breeds from tree limit in Canada to northern tier of states and down mountains to North Carolina, preferring coniferous forests. Winters in southern part of this range, and occasionally as far as Gulf states. *Distinguished by black cap, black eye streak through white face and neck, and reddish-brown belly and breast.* A more nasal "yahnk-yahnk" cry than above bird's. May use wren-size bird box hidden among tree branches.

121. BROWN-HEADED NUTHATCH *(Sitta pusilla)*. 4-5". Resident from southern Missouri, Kentucky, and Delaware to Gulf states and Florida, usually in open pine woods. *The brown cap on head and the sharply contrasting grayish-blue back and white under parts are distinctive.* A shrill "kit-kit-kit" call repeated rapidly; also has shrill piping squeak like "kee-day" or "kee-dee-dee," repeated frequently; and may chatter or twitter. Usually digs own nest in dead wood, but may come to nest box.

122. BROWN CREEPER *(Certhia familiaris)*. 5-6". Breeds from southern Canada to northern states and down mountains to North Carolina; winters in warmer parts of the country down to Florida and Gulf states. Likes woodlands. *Instantly identified by the way it spirals up a trunk probing for insects and using its stiff tail for a prop, then flies to bottom of next tree to repeat process.* Usually calls with long weak "seeeeeeee" note. Song has a lot of high "tee-see" and "see" notes. Also eats pine nuts and corn. Generally nests from 5-15' up under curling or rotting bark.

123. GOLDEN-CROWNED KINGLET *(Regulus satrapa)*. 3½-4". Breeds from southern Canada to northern tier of states and through mountains to North Carolina, preferring coniferous forests, especially spruces; winters in woods over same general area and south to Gulf states and northern Florida. *Main distinguishing mark is a bright crown, orange in male, yellow in female;* otherwise this bird of small size and dark colors might go unnoticed among

tangles of twigs. The high-pitched wiry "see-see-see" call is distinctive. King-lets constantly flick wings as they hop about among branchlets. Generally nests high in concealed places in spruce trees. Eats mainly upon insects.

124. RUBY-CROWNED KINGLET *(Regulus calendula)*. 3½-4½". Breeds mainly in Canadian spruce forests; migrates through northern states, and winters in woods from Iowa and Virginia southward. *The tiny size; broken, white eye-ring; quick flitting movements and, general olive-gray colors are characteristic;* the bright red crown patch in the male is rarely seen. Differs from warblers by having a shorter tail, and a black wing bar behind the white one. Feeds mainly on insects.

Most thrushes are fine singers. They eat berries and other fruit, also come to suet and eat seeds and insect mix. Bluebirds will nest in bluebird-type houses, while other thrushes prefer robin-type, open box nests.

THRUSHES AND VIREOS

125. ROBIN *(Turdus migratorius)*. 8½-10½". Breeds from northern Canada to Georgia and northern areas of the Gulf states; winters from Ohio Valley and New England coast southward. Likes open wooded areas. *The brick-red breast and the yellow bill are distinctive;* young birds have speckled breasts and are reddish on the sides. Song is formed in groups of two or three clear, whistled notes. Likes insects, earthworms, and various wild and cultivated fruits.

126. WOOD THRUSH *(Hylocichla mustelina)*. 7½-8½". Breeds from central Minnesota and Michigan, southern Ontario, New York, and southern Maine to Gulf states and northern Florida; winters from Florida south, preferring broad-leaved woodlands. *Has distinctive rusty head; also spots on belly and breast are quite large and round.* Song has several flute-like rounded phrases, one part sounding like "ee-yo-lay"; also has gargled notes, and fast "pit-pip-pit-pit" call. Eats insects and wild fruits.

127. HERMIT THRUSH *(Hylocichla guttata)*. 6½-7½". Breeds from south-ern Canada to northern tier of states, and in mountains to Virginia, frequenting mixed evergreen and broad-leaved woods; winters from Connecticut and Ohio Valley to Gulf Coast and Florida. *Reddish-brown tail and rump and numerous reddish-brown to brown spots on breast are distinctive.* Has very beautiful song of flute-like phrases, each climbing in pitch. A "whit" note. Feeds on insects and wild fruits of holly, dogwood, and various bushes.

128. OLIVE-BACKED THRUSH *(Hylocichla ustulata)*. 6½-7½". Breeds in spruce forests of Canada and southward inland to the northern border of the United States; migrates through southern states; winters in tropics. *With a back of plain olive-brown and a brown-streaked breast, this bird is similar to the Gray-cheeked Thrush and is distinguished only by the yellowish-brown eye ring.* The flute-like phrases of the song form light melodies, each rising in pitch. A sweet "phit, phit" note. Eats insects, spiders, snails, and such various wild fruits as of cherry, dogwood, elderberry.

129. GRAY-CHEEKED THRUSH *(Hylocichla minima)*. 6½-8". Breeds in spruce forests from limit of trees in Canada to mountains of New York and New England; winters in tropics. Very similar to the Olive-backed Thrush but has

NUTHATCHES, CREEPER, AND KINGLETS

120. RED-BREASTED NUTHATCH

♀

124. RUBY-CROWNED KINGI

♂

119. WHITE-BREASTED
NUTHATCH

121. BROWN-HEADED NUTHATCH

122. BROWN CREEI

123. GOLDEN-CROWNED KINGLET

♀   ♂

Rosinda Holmes

THRUSHES AND BLUE BIRDS

125. ROBIN

126. WOOD THRUSH

127. HERMIT THRUSH

128. OLIVE-BACKED THRUSH

129. GRAY-CHEEKED THRUSH

130. VEERY

immature

131. EASTERN BLUEBIRD

gray cheeks and lacks the eye-ring. Weak nasal song has sharp rise in pitch at close; has shrill nasal "veee-ah" or "zueeeah" note. Eats insects, crayfish, and the fruits of dogwood, cherry, and other plants.

130. **VEERY** *(Hylocichla fuscescens).* 6½-7½″. Breeds from Newfoundland and southern Canada to Iowa, Ohio, New Jersey, and through the mountains to northern Georgia, in well-shaded woods; winters in tropics. *All over reddish- or yellowish-brown,* sparsely marked with light spots on breast. The light liquid whistle spirals downward in pitch, as "vee-yur, vee-yr, vee, veer.' A "pew" note. Eats insects and fruits.

131. **EASTERN BLUEBIRD** *(Sialia sialis).* 6½-7½″. Breeds from southern Canada to Gulf states and Florida, frequenting such areas as open woods, brushy fields, farms, and gardens. *It is the only red-breasted blue bird;* female duller; young birds mostly brownish and speckled but with some blue in wings and tail. Has soft sweet "tur-wee" note, and a gurgling song of three to four notes. Eats insects and fleshy fruits.

VIREOS

Vireos are small plain-colored birds, secretive, and slow-moving among small branches of trees. They feed on insects and nest in bushes or trees. Small robin-type houses might attract them, and they may be attracted with suet, insect mix, and fleshy fruits.

132. **WHITE-EYED VIREO** *(Vireo griseus).* 4½-5½″. Breeds from southern Minnesota and Michigan, central New York and Massachusetts, and southward to Gulf states and northern Florida, mainly in brushy areas; winters from South Carolina and Gulf states south. Vireos look very much alike, but this one is identified by *whitish throat, yellowish spectacles, and white eyes.* Song is not vireo-like, but a "tik-ah-peer-weoo-tik" sharply-uttered.

133. **BELL'S VIREO** *(Vireo bellii).* 4½-5″. Breeds from Illinois and southern Minnesota to Arkansas, mainly west of Mississippi River and in streamside woods; winters from Texas south. *The most plain-colored of the vireos, it is mostly grayish with faded whitish wing bars; similar to the White-eyed Vireo, but has dark eyes.* Not much music in soft, husky "seedle, seedle, shee? seedle, seedle, shew!" song, like a question and an answer.

134. **YELLOW-THROATED VIREO** *(Vireo flavifrons).* 5-6″. Breeds from southern Canada to the Gulf states and northern Florida; winters in tropics; likes deciduous woods and parks. *Only vireo with bright yellow throat and sides; has white wing bars and yellowish spectacles.* Sings repeated, low-pitched, musical "teebrrr, teebrrrr" with short pauses between phrases. One phrase may sound like "tee-yate."

135. **BLUE-HEADED VIREO,** or **SOLITARY VIREO** *(Vireo solitarius).* 5-6″. Breeds in mixed coniferous and deciduous forests from southern Canada to northern tier of states, and through mountains to northern Georgia; winters from South Carolina through Florida and Gulf states. Appears much like White-eyed Vireo, but *has black eyes, blue-gray head, eye-ring,* and throat is more snowy white. Song is a series of short whistles, undulating in pitch, with pauses between phrases, higher and sweeter and more slurring in tone than song of Red-eyed Vireo.

136. **RED-EYED VIREO** *(Vireo olivaceus)*. 5½-6½". Breeds from southern Canada to Gulf states and central Florida; winters in tropics. Inhabits deciduous woods. *Has no wing bars, but has a gray cap and a very sharply marked, black-edged white stripe over each red eye.* Song rather monotonously repeated quick phrases, each with a short pause between, sung about 35-40 phrases per minute.

137. **PHILADELPHIA VIREO** *(Vireo philadelphicus)*. 4½-5". Breeds from southern Canada to northern border of the United States, in broad-leaf woods and edges of clearings; winters in Central America. *The only vireo that has both plain unbarred wings and a dull yellowish belly and breast;* there is often a dark spot behind. Song like that of the Red-eyed Vireo but is shriller and less frequently repeated.

138. **WARBLING VIREO** *(Vireo gilvus)*. 5-6". Breeds in tall, broad-leaved trees from southern Canada to Louisiana, western Tennessee, and North Carolina; winters in tropics. *Very much like the Philadelphia Vireo, as both lack wing-bars and the head is not conspicuously striped like that of the Red-eyed. The Warbling Vireo differs in having a whitish breast.* Sings a rather sleepy, liquid warble, without the broken phrases of other vireos; it consists of rolling "rrrrrs" and a sharp "pit" at the end; also a wheezy "tzwee" call.

WOOD WARBLERS

Warblers, excepting the Chat, are mostly smaller than sparrows and are brightly-colored (usually with some yellow), actively flitting birds, with very thin bills. Most of them live on insects and will come to suet. A few may nest in chickadee-type bird houses. Note that the Yellow-throated Vireo and Ruby-crowned Kinglet look very much like warblers.

139. **WORM-EATING WARBLER** *(Helmitheros vermivorus)*. 5-5½". Breeds from southern Iowa, Ohio, and Connecticut to Missouri and northern Georgia, mainly in broad-leaved woods. *Yellowish-brown on top of head and black stripes on sides are distinctive.* Very thin buzzy rattling song, like the chirp of a cricket.

140. **SWAINSON'S WARBLER** *(Limnothlypis swainsonii)*. 4¾-5¼". Found from southern Missouri and Virginia to the Gulf states and northern Florida. It is seldom seen in the wooded cane swamps it frequents, but often heard is its song, *beginning with two slurred notes, dropping in pitch, then swinging higher on the last of the five note tune. The olive-to-reddish-brown crown has a black stripe below it.*

141. **LOUISIANA WATER THRUSH** *(Seiurus motacilla)*. 6-6¼". Breeds from southern New Hampshire, southern Michigan, and southeastern Minnesota to northern areas of the Gulf states, northern Georgia, and central South Carolina. Habitat is brushy ravines and streamside woods of hills and mountains, rarely in swamps.

Both water thrushes are brown-backed birds with light streaks over the eyes and brown-streaked underparts, but only the Louisiana Water Thrush has a *white throat, white eye-stripe, and white belly.* Song starts with three sharp, but slurred whistles, followed by a jumble of down-pitching twitters.

132. WHITE-EYED VIREO

133. BELL'S VIREO

134. YELLOW-THROATED VIREO

135. BLUE-HEADED or SOLITARY VIREO

137. PHILADELPHIA VIREO

136. RED-EYED VIREO

138. WARBLING VIREO

Rosinda Holmes

WARBLERS

139. WORM-EATING WARBLER

144. TENNESEE WARBLER

♂

140. SWAINSON'S WARBLER

141. LOUISIANA WATER THRUSH

143. OVEN BIRD

145. BLACK AND WHITE WARBLER

♂

142. NORTHERN WATER THRUSH

♀

146. YELLOW-THROATED WARBLER

♂

142. NORTHERN WATER THRUSH *(Seiurus noveboracensis)*. 5-6". Breeds from tree limit in Canada to northern tier of states and through the mountains to West Virginia, frequenting wooded swamps and swamplike edges of streams. Similar to preceding bird, but has *yellowish eye-streak, throat, breast, and belly.* The song is a rapid stutter, then drops at end to "shew-shew-shew" notes.

143. OVEN BIRD *(Seiurus aurocapillus)*. 5½-6½". Breeds from southern Canada to Arkansas and northern Georgia, preferring leafy litter on floor of broad-leaved woods; winters from Florida and Gulf Coast south. *Identified by orange crown, pink legs, and white eye ring; better still by loud, startling "teecher, teecher, teecher"* or *"ter-chea, ter-chea, ter-chea" song.*

144. TENNESSEE WARBLER *(Vermivora peregrina)*. 4½-5". Breeds from southern Canada to northern tier of states; migrates mainly through Mississippi Valley; winters in tropics; frequents spruce and tamarack swamps. *In spring it is recognized by gray crown, white eye stripe, and white breast; in fall it is much plainer, and is best identified by white under-tail coverts, pale yellow wing stripe, and green back.*

145. BLACK AND WHITE WARBLER *(Mniotilta varia)*. 5-5½". Breeds from southern Canada to northern edge of Gulf states, in broad-leaved woods; winters from Florida south. *Very distinctive black and white streaked design;* it has solid black head cap similar to that of the Blackpoll Warbler, 169, which it resembles. Song of frequently repeated sibilant "whee-see, whee-see" phrases, with second note lower than first.

146. YELLOW-THROATED WARBLER *(Dendroica dominica)*. 5-5½". Breeds in Atlantic coastal lowlands from New Jersey to Florida, and from southern Michigan and Wisconsin to the Gulf states, frequenting pines, live oaks, and sycamores; winters from Gulf states and Florida into the tropics. *Distinctive yellow throat and gray back.*

WOOD WARBLERS

147. ORANGE CROWNED WARBLER *(Vermivora celata)*. 4¾-5¼". Breeds in western Canada, but migrates through Mississippi Valley, wintering in Gulf and south Atlantic states, rarely as far north as New York, liking brushy places. *The dullest-colored of all warblers, rarely showing reddish-orange crown, has no wing-bars, but has faint streaks on breast.* A very weak, plain, somewhat burry trill for a song.

148. YELLOW-BREASTED CHAT *(Icteria virens)*. 7-7½". Breeds from southern Ontario and northern tier of states, except northern New England, southward to Gulf states and Florida; likes thorny thickets and clearings in brush. *The only very large warbler, showing long tail, green back, white spectacles, and yellow breast.* Has distinctive song of mixed soft "caws," harsh notes, and clear whistles.

149. PARULA WARBLER *(Parula americana)*. 4¼-4¾". Breeds from southern Canada to the Gulf States and Florida, preferring damp woodlands, especially those hung with Spanish moss; winters in Florida and further south. *The blue general color, and yellow throat and breast are distinctive; a dark band across breast of male is characteristic.* Usual song is a buzzing, rattling trill like "zzzzeeeeeeeee-ip."

48

150. BLACK-THROATED BLUE WARBLER *(Dendroica coerulescens)*. 5-5½″. Breeds from southern Canada to northern tier of states and in mountains to northern Georgia; winters in tropics. *The male is quite unique, with its blackish-blue throat and sides, and blue back, but female is a nondescript olive-green except for distinctive dark cheeks and a white blotch on wing border;* most young birds are even duller, and lack the white blotch. Has husky, sleepy-sounding "zrr-zrr-zrr-zrreeeee" song.

151. MOURNING WARBLER *(Oporornis philadelphia)*. 5-5¾″. Breeds from southern Canada into northern tier of states and through the mountains to West Virginia; migrates mainly west of mountains; winters in tropics. Likes swamp-like thickets and clearings surrounded by brush. There are several gray-hooded warblers, but the *male of this species has a distinctive black throat,* and the young and female (especially in fall) has incomplete white eye-rings (obscured in front). Very ringing, variable song, often sounding like "cheery, cheery, churry, churry."

152. YELLOW-THROAT *(Geothlypis trichas)*. 4½-5½″. Breeds from central and southern Canada to the Gulf states and Florida; winters from North Carolina and Gulf states southward, preferring low, swampy, or damp, brushy areas. *Male is instantly recognized by striking black mask; the female and young have yellow throat in combination with the white belly.* Song a rather remarkable repetition of sharp "whichity-whitchity" notes.

153. PROTHONOTARY WARBLER *(Prothonotaria citrea)*. 5¼-5¾″. Breeds from southern Minnesota, southern Michigan, Ohio, and southern New Jersey to Gulf states and central Florida; winters in tropics; likes swampy river areas. *Distinctive golden orange on head, throat, and breast; male has bluish wings; female is duller with gray wings.* Song is sharply-repeated "tveet" or "tweet" notes of level tone.

154. NASHVILLE WARBLER *(Vermivora ruficapilla)*. 4½-5″. Breeds from southern Canada to northern states and through mountains to West Virginia; migrates to tropics. Frequents cut-over land and fringes of bogs. *The yellow under-parts, especially bright on throat, and the white eye-ring are best distinguishing marks.* Song starts as "see-blit, see-blit" and ends in a sustained high trill.

WOOD WARBLERS

155. KENTUCKY WARBLER *(Oporornis formosus)*. 5¼-5¾″. From Iowa, southern Michigan, and southern New York to Gulf states and Florida; winters in tropics; likes broad-leaved woods. *Has distinctive yellow eye-ring spectacles and black throat blotches or sideburns.* The characteristic rolling, rapidly-voiced "chory-chory-chory" is heard while the shy bird is usually unseen.

156. HOODED WARBLER *(Wilsonia citrina)*. 5-5¾″. Breeds from Iowa, southern Michigan, Ohio, and Rhode Island to Gulf states and Florida; winters in tropics. Likes wooded swamps and underbrush and thickets of broad-leaved woodlands. *Male is easily identified by the black hood enclosing the yellow face; female and young are plainer, but bright yellow face and white spots on tail are distinctive. Tail nervously and rapidly opened and folded, showing white spots.* Very loudly whistled clear song of five to eleven notes, sounding like "taweet, taweet-tee-too," the last note slurred.

148. YELLOW-BREASTED CHAT

147. ORANGE CROWNED
WARBLER

150. BLACK-THROATED BLUE WARBLER

♀

♂

149. PARULA
WARBLER

♀ ♂

♀

♂

151. MOURNING WARBLER

152. YELLOW-THROAT

♀

♂

153. PROTHONOTARY WARBLER

Rosindo
Holmes

WARBLERS OF UNUSUAL COLORS, LARGE SIZE, OR PLAIN COLORS

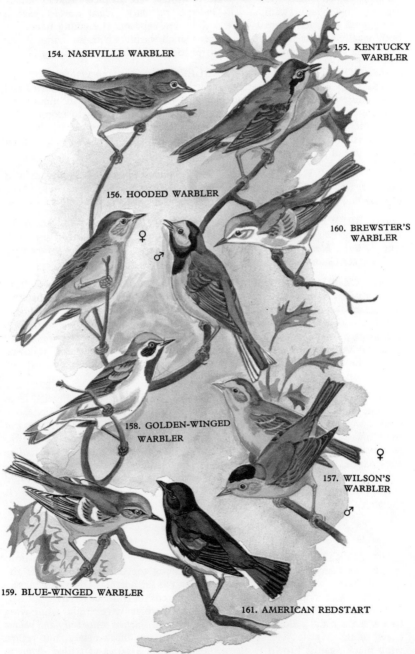

154. NASHVILLE WARBLER

155. KENTUCKY WARBLER

156. HOODED WARBLER

160. BREWSTER'S WARBLER

158. GOLDEN-WINGED WARBLER

157. WILSON'S WARBLER

159. BLUE-WINGED WARBLER

161. AMERICAN REDSTART

157. WILSON'S WARBLER *(Wilsonia pusilla).* 4½-5". Breeds from central Canada to northern tier of states; winters in tropics. Likes brushy areas in bogs and swamps. *The male is the only yellow warbler with a round black cap;* female may show a dull dark cap, and the young none, but both usually appear as very plain-colored small warblers with no marks of any kind. Has very staccato, bright and emphatic "vititittititititetoo" song.

158. GOLDEN-WINGED WARBLER *(Vermivora chrysoptera).* 5-5¼". Breeds from southern Minnesota, central Michigan, southern Ontario, and Massachusetts to Missouri, Indiana, and northern Georgia in mountains, avoiding south Atlantic coast; migrates through Gulf states to tropics. *The combination of yellow wing patch and black throat are characteristic;* black colors are grayish in female. Song a very distinctive, but light "zeez-zz-zz-zz" similar to the buzz of an insect.

159. BLUE-WINGED WARBLER *(Vermivora pinus).* 5½-5". Breeds over same area as the Golden-winged Warbler. Distinguished by narrow, black, eye-bar and yellow undersides. "See-zuzzzz" song usually has only two notes.

160. BREWSTER'S WARBLER *(Vermivora leucobronchialis).* About 5". Range as of two preceding birds, and probably a cross between these species since *it has a black, thin eye-bar like the Blue-winged Warbler, but yellow wing bars like the Golden-winged one.*

161. AMERICAN REDSTART *(Setophaga ruticilla).* 4½-5½". Breeds from southern Canada to northern Georgia and northern borders of the Gulf states; winters in the tropics. Frequents medium-sized, broad-leaved trees. *Male is only bird with all over black above, except for bright orange patches, and white belly and breast; female marked by distinctive yellow tail and side patches contrasted with grayish-green back and wings.* Songs usually begin "seet-seet-seet" followed by "tseeta-seeta-seeta" phrases, ending either in downward slur, a high-pitched note, or on same level.

162. CERULEAN WARBLER *(Dendroica cerulea).* 4-5". Breeds from western New York, southern Ontario, Wisconsin, and southern Minnesota, mainly west of Appalachian crest, to northern Georgia and northern areas of the Gulf states; winters in tropics. Frequents river valley woods. *Though the blue and white colors of male are distinctive, a bird high in a tree is best told by black bar between white throat and breast.* The female is more greenish or bluish-gray above and whitish below with two white wing bars on gray wings. A rapid single-pitched trilling "zay-zay-zay" followed by higher pitched "bzeeeee" is the song.

WOOD WARBLERS

163. MYRTLE WARBLER *(Dendroica coronata).* 5-6". Breeds from limit of trees in Canada to Massachusetts and along the northern border of the United States; winters in southern states and as far north as Ohio and Massachusetts. Likes coniferous forests, and often feeds on fruits of bayberry, cedar, and poison ivy. The Cape May and Magnolia Warblers have similar white wing bars and black and yellow markings, but not the *distinctive white belly and yellow crown* of the Myrtle Warbler. Females are without black marks, but yellow wing patch against brown is characteristic. Sings a series of trilled seven to twenty-one sharp, rapid and colorless, rather weak notes, fewer in springtime.

52

164. MAGNOLIA WARBLER *(Dendroica magnolia)*. 4½-5¼″. Breeds from central Canada and Newfoundland to Massachusetts, through the mountains to Virginia, eastern Ohio, northern Michigan, and Minnesota; winters in tropics; likes young coniferous forests. The *wide black band at end of tail, and immediately preceding white bands are the most characteristic marks;* note also large white blotch on wing and heavy black streaks on yellow breast; the young bird in fall does not have these streaks. The only warbler in evergreen woods that has a "veeta veeta veeta" song.

165. CANADA WARBLER *(Wilsonia canadensis)*. 5-5¾″. Breeds from southern Canada to northern tier of states and through the mountains to northern Georgia; winters in tropics; likes underbrush in woods. *Distinctive necklace of short black streaks on breast;* in female and young these marks are less distinct, but all have *yellow-eye* spectacles. A very loud and striking, irregular, and variously pitched song.

166. CHESTNUT-SIDED WARBLER *(Dendroica pensylvanica)*. 4¾-5″. Breeds from southern Canada to Iowa, Indiana, Pennsylvania, and through mountains to Tennessee and South Carolina; winters in tropics. Likes brushy, cut-over forest and pastures. *The bright chestnut-red sides, yellow crown, and black narrow side-burns are distinctive.* Young in fall are quite different, being white beneath and yellow-green above, with yellow wing bars. Has two kinds of chattering non-musical songs, one sounding like "vera vera pleasta-meetcha," the other more variable.

167. CAPE MAY WARBLER *(Dendroica tigrina)*. 5-5½″. Breeds throughout much of central and eastern Canada and northern New England; winters in West Indies. The only warbler with reddish-brown cheeks; both sexes have tiger-like blackish-brown stripes on yellow front; young and female have yellowish or whitish neck blotches. Very thin, wiry, sibilant "see-see-see-see" song, repeated often.

168. PRAIRIE WARBLER *(Dendroica discolor)*. 4½-5″. Breeds from Iowa, southern Michigan, Ohio, and Massachusetts to Gulf states and Florida; winters in Florida and West Indies. Likes dry, scrubby pine and oak areas, cut-over or burned. *Black stripes appear on yellow sides only, two black face stripes on yellow face;* young birds duller; *all wag tails vigorously.* Clear, sharp, thin, sibilant, distinctly separated and rising "zee" notes in song.

168a. CONNECTICUT WARBLER, *Oporornis agilis*. This is one of three gray-hooded orioles in our region, but the lack of dark markings on the throat of the male and the comparatively dark brownish-green-yellow back, wings and tail are fairly distinctive, also somewhat larger size. It is a summer visitor to the northeastern coniferous forests of Canada, Minnesota, Michigan, and Wisconsin, but rare farther east.

169. BLACKPOLL WARBLER *(Dendroica striata)*. 5-5¼″. Breeds from tree limit in Canada to northern tier of states; migrates through eastern states to South America. *The solid black on top of head and black side stripes of male are distinctive;* female is more nondescriptly striped; all birds in fall appear striped on brown above and on greenish below, with *white under tail.* High, thin, insect-like song.

WOOD WARBLERS

170. BLACK-THROATED GREEN WARBLER *(Dendroica virens)*. 4½-5¼″. Breeds from southern Canada south to Minnesota, northern Michigan, Long Island, New Jersey, and through mountains to South Carolina; winters in

162. CERULEAN WARBLER ♂ ♀

163. MYRTLE WARBLER ♀ ♂

164. MAGNOLIA WARBLER ♂ ♀

165. CANADA WARBLER ♀ ♂

167. CAPE MAY WARBLER ♀ ♂

166. CHESTNUT-SIDED WARBLER ♂

168a. CONNECTICUT WARBLER ♂ ♀

168. PRAIRIE WARBLER ♂

Rosinda Holmes

169. BLACKPOLL WARBLER

♀ ♂

170. BLACK-THROATED GREEN WARBLER

immature

♂

174. BAY-BREASTED WARBLER

171. PALM WARBLER

♂

172. YELLOW WARBLER

♀ immature

♂ ♀

175. PINE WARBLER

173. BLACKBURNIAN WARBLER

tropics. Frequents coniferous woods. *The bright yellow face has a black throat below and an olive-green back and crown above in male;* female is similar but with much less black; young have dusky streaks on throat below yellow cheeks. The very sweet, musical "zree zree zree-zree troo zree" song is sometimes in three pitches. Another and similar song has first note three times as long as last note.

171. PALM WARBLER *(Dendroica palmarum)*. 5-5½". Breeds from southern Canada to the northern border of the United States; winters in southernmost states, but occasionally north along coast to Massachusetts. Frequents boggy places, and is found mainly on ground. *It is the only warbler in this habitat that flicks tail up and down. In spring and summer it can also be recognized by its reddish-brown cap and black streak through eye;* later it becomes duller in color. Song a musical short trill or repeated trills with slight up and down pitch.

172. YELLOW WARBLER *(Dendroica petechia)*. 4¾-5¼". *Breeds among willows near water from southern Canada* to Missouri, northern Georgia, and western South Carolina; a sub-species lives in mangrove swamps of Florida Keys; winters in tropics. *This is the only small bird that appears all yellow from a distance,* though a closer look reveals some black on wings and tail, and reddish streaks on undersides of male. Both sexes have yellow spots on tail. Song has slightly sibilant musical "tsee-tzee" notes.

173. BLACKBURNIAN WARBLER *(Dendroica fusca)*. 5-5½". Breeds from southern Canada to northern tier of states and through the mountains to northern Georgia; winters in tropics. *Male has flaming orange on throat and head, with black markings;* female is more yellowish; young birds have yellow throats, dark cheeks, and striped, dark grayish and whitish backs. Song distinctively single or double-noted at first, followed by very high pitched trill.

174. BAY-BREASTED WARBLER *(Dendroica castanea)*. 5-6". Breeds from southern Canada south to north edge of United States; migrates throughout east; winters in tropics. Frequents dense spruce forests. *The pale, pinkish neck blotch contrasts sharply with the chestnut-red of crown and breast and the wide black eye mark in the male;* female is similar but with pale reddish coloring on breast; in the fall, both adults lose bright colors except for some reddish on sides of belly. The young Bay-breasted and the fall Blackpoll (169) are both grayish-green-brown birds with whitish wing bars and streaked underparts, but the streaks are heavier in the Blackpoll. A short sibilant shrill song is heard, but with uneven mixture of short and long "tsee-tseelee-lee-te te teeee" notes.

175. PINE WARBLER *(Dendroica pinus)*. 5-5¼". Breeds from southern Canada to Gulf states and Florida; winters from southern Illinois through southern states; frequents open pine woods. *The rather vague gray-brown streaking on the lemon-yellow breast, the white wing bars, and the white belly are distinctive.* Female is more dull-colored; the young resemble the Bay-breasted and Blackpoll Warblers in fall, with their plain greenish-olive-brown colors, but it has no streaks on back. *Creeps over pine trunks and large branches, much like a creeper;* eats pine nuts. Song a musical trill or series of rapid high notes.

STARLING, MEADOWLARKS, BLACKBIRDS, BOBOLINK, AND ORIOLES

Birds of this group have general purpose, long, medium-thick bills adapted for feeding on such varied foods as insects, seeds, and berries. Some may nest in robin-type nest boxes.

176. STARLING *(Sturnus vulgaris)*. 7½-8½". Resident in most of our region in farms, towns, and cities. *Resembles a short-tailed blackbird, glittering with purple and green in the spring, speckled with small pale dots in the winter; yellow spike-like bill is also distinctive.* Song a mixture of whistled musical and harsh and rasping notes; shrill "tseee-oo" call.

177. EASTERN MEADLOWLARK *(Sturnella magma)*. 9-11". Breeds from southern Canada and eastern Minnesota to Florida and the Gulf states; winters mainly in southern states. *A stocky, brown bird with short, wide tail bordered with white; the yellow breast is crossed by black "V" marks.* Two clear, musical but slurred whistles resembling "heeta-oyear" or "ahseet-ayair" are its song. WESTERN MEADOWLARK *(Sturnella neglecta)* is similar to the eastern species; found on western edge of our region, and is recognized by a longer, gurgling song.

178. YELLOW-HEADED BLACKBIRD *(Xanthocephalus xanthocephalus)*. 9-11". Breeds from central Canada to Iowa and northern Indiana; winters from western Louisiana to Mexico, prefers marshes. *The male is immediately identified by yellow head and black body;* female browner and has a white streaked breast and yellow throat. Has "krik" or "krak" note song that is file-like and rasping as the squeaking of an old hinge.

179. BOBOLINK *(Dolichonyx oryzivorus)*. 6½-8". Breeds from southern Canada to northern states; migrates to tropics. Frequents meadows. *In spring, the male has unique pattern of black below and is mainly white above;* in autumn the male has brown streaks on yellowish breast, and whitish yellow head with dark stripes, the all-seasons coloring of the female. A bubbling, cheerful, melodious, upward pitching song, given in flight; a "pink" call.

180. RED-WINGED BLACKBIRD *(Agelaius phoeniceus)*. 7½-9½". Breeds in marshes and swamps from southern Canada to Florida and the Gulf states; winters mainly in southern states. *The bright red wing patches of the black male are very distinctive;* female and young are heavily striped with brown. A liquid "kleak-lay—reeeee" song. (See other blackbirds 63, 64, 65.)

181. ORCHARD ORIOLE *(Icterus spurius)*. 6-7¼". Breeds from Minnesota, southeast Ontario, and southern New England to the Gulf states and Florida in farmed or fallow open country; winters in tropics. *Male is dark chestnut and black, with the all-black tail distinguishing it from the Baltimore Oriole;* young male is yellowish with black throat stripe; female is olive-drab on upper surfaces and a dull yellowish tone below. Song very rapid spurt of flute-like whistles and gargled notes, happy in sound; also a shrill pausing "whit-cheer" call.

182. BALTIMORE ORIOLE *(Icterus galbula)*. 7-8". Breeds from southern Canada to northern Georgia and northern areas of the Gulf states; winters in tropics. Male is blazing orange and black; an occasional female is a pale version of the male but the usual coloring is brownish and yellowish. Song of rich, vigorous, varied and irregular notes, often with each note going sharply downward in pitch, also a low "hew-lee" whistle.

Tanagers are mainly insect eaters, but feed also on various wild fruits and berries. Usually nest fairly high in trees; might use robin-type nest box.

183. SCARLET TANAGER *(Piranga olivacea)*. 6½-7½". Breeds from southern Canada to Arkansas, northern Alabama, and northern Georgia, avoiding

BLACKBIRDS, ORIOLES, MEADOWLARK, AND BOBOLINK

176. STARLING

177. EASTERN
MEADOWLARK

179. BOBOLINK
♂
♀

178. YELLOW-HEADED
BLACKBIRD
♂

181. ORCHARD ORIOLE
♂
♀

180. RED-WINGED
BLACKBIRD
♂

182. BALTIMORE
ORIOLE
♂
♀

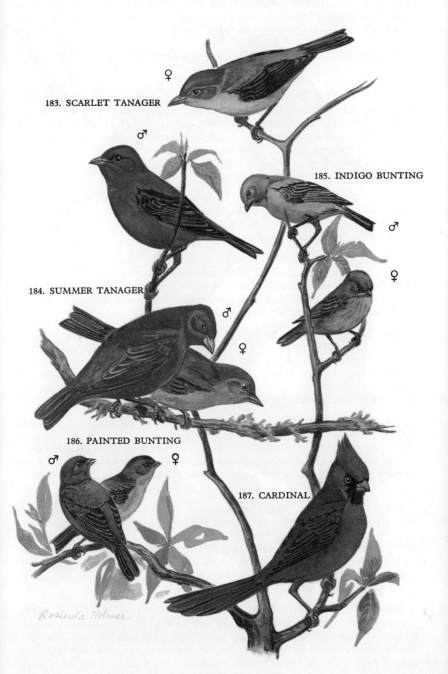

183. SCARLET TANAGER

185. INDIGO BUNTING

184. SUMMER TANAGER

186. PAINTED BUNTING

187. CARDINAL

Rosinda Holmes

Atlantic coastal plain, but migrates through this area and southward to tropics. Frequents broadleaved woodlands. *Breeding male is a distinctive bright scarlet with black wings and tail;* female is a plain yellowish and olive-brown. The song is a husky, squeaking and file-like "chuk" note.

TANAGER, BUNTINGS, DICKCISSEL, GROSBEAK, AND PURPLE FINCH

184. SUMMER TANAGER *(Piranga rubra)*. 7-7½". Breeds from southern Iowa, southern Wisconsin, central Ohio, and Delaware to Florida and the Gulf states; winters in the tropics. Frequents oak and other broad-leaved woodlands. *Males are a solid, bright rose-red;* females are a bright yellowish below and have a lighter greenish yellow above than similar Scarlet Tanager females. A varied, loud, liquid, series of notes like "pah-chip-it, tuck-tuck" or "hee-parah-vee-yer-chuwit-tahwee" is the song.

The concluding discussion is on birds of the finch family; they have *thick short bills* suited for seed eating, but most species also eat berries and insects and will come to suet and bird seed mix. Some will nest in wren or blue-bird size houses, or small size open robin-type houses.

185. INDIGO BUNTING *(Passerina cyanea)*. 5¼-5¾". Breeds from southern Canada to middle areas of the Gulf states and Georgia; winters in tropics. *Males are a very rich, beautiful blue all over, losing some blue in fall;* females are a plain brown with faint wing-bars. Very high, shrill song, with notes such as "seet-seet, twi-tew" usually sung in pairs.

186. PAINTED BUNTING *(Passerina ciris)*. 5-5½". Breeds from Arkansas and southeast North Carolina through lowlands of the Gulf states and Florida; winters from Florida and southern Louisiana into tropics. Frequents bushes of towns and open areas. *Male is a fantastic mixture of bright red, green, and dark blue; female is the only all green finch.* Song a dry, wiry, but musical warble; has "chip" note. Prefers bristlegrass seeds.

187. CARDINAL *(Richmondena cardinalis)*. 8-9". Resident from southern Minnesota, southern Ontario, and southern New York to Florida and the Gulf states. *No other male bird is all red and crested; the female is brownish but has a red bill and crest.* The clear but slurred whistles of the song gradually go down in pitch, and "what-cheer, cheer-cheer" and "Quoit-quoit-quoit" are among verbalized simulations.

188. DICKCISSEL *(Spiza americana)*. 6-7". Breeds in midwest from western Ohio to southeast Ontario and southern Michigan and southward to western Alabama and Louisiana; winters in tropics. Inhabits grasslands. *The yellow breast, black throat, and white eye streak on gray head of male are characteristic;* female is of duller coloring, streaked body and face and a bluish bill. Song comes in machine-gun-like bursts of "dik-siss-siss", or "kup-kulp-klip-klip" repeatedly uttered.

189. EVENING GROSBEAK *(Hesperiphona vespertina)*. 7½-8½". Breeds in spruce forests of northeastern Canada and westward to northern Michigan; winters occasionally east and south into Virginia, Kentucky, and Missouri. *Easily distinguished by very large, cone-shaped white bill, and dark yellowish general coloring; male has distinctive yellow and black on head and large white*

wing patches; female has distinctive white streaks in black tail and is more grayish-yellow on breast. Feeds on many insects, but also feeds on maple, dogwood, cherry, and other fruits. Very short irregular, warbling song. Sharp, ringing "cleer-lip" call note.

190. PURPLE FINCH *(Carpodacus purpureus).* 5½-6¼". Breeds from Newfoundland and southern Canada to central Minnesota, northern Indiana, and Long Island, and in mountains down to Maryland. Winters from southern Ontario and Minnesota and from New England to the Gulf states and Florida. *Male is bright rosy-red on head and rump, lighter rose on breast and back;* has white belly, and is brown-streaked elsewhere; the female is an entirely brown and white-streaked bird. Song, a cheerful, rapid, warble; has metallic "pik" note.

GROSBEAKS, SISKIN, GOLDFINCH, CROSSBILLS, AND TOWHEE

191. PINE GROSBEAK *(Pinicola enucleator).* 9-10". Breeds in coniferous forests from near tree limit in Canada to New England mountains; winters occasionally in southern states. *The unusually long tail and robin-size are characteristic; rosy all over except black wings and tail; yellowish-brown above except for black wings and tail, whitish below and has light eye stripe and dark jaw stripe.* Eats pine nuts, and fruits of blackberries, red cedar, mountain maple, and other plants. Clear "tee-tee-tu" whistle.

192. BLUE GROSBEAK *(Guiraca caerulea).* 6½-7½". Breeds from Missouri, southern Ohio, and Maryland to the Gulf states and Florida; winters in tropics. Likes bushy areas and willow thickets. *Male is a rather dull blue with reddish-brown wing bars and markings; female is mainly brown and tan. Heavy bill* is adapted to feeding on insects, wheat, and seeds such as those of bristlegrass and panicgrass. Has low gutteral rapid warble.

193. ROSE-BREASTED GROSBEAK *(Pheucticus ludovicianus).* 7-8½". Breeds from southern Canada to Missouri, central Ohio, New Jersey, and through the mountains to northern Georgia; frequents second-growth, broad-leaved woods; winters in tropics. *The unique combination of rose-red breast with black and white characterizes the male;* the female has brown and white head streaks and broad white wing-bars. Eats insects, wild fruits, and seeds. Mellow, robin-like song.

194. PINE SISKIN *(Spinus pinus).* 4½-5". Breeds in coniferous forests from near tree limit in Canada to northern border of United States and through mountains to North Carolina; winters widely but spottily throughout the United States. *The small size, heavy brown streaking, and flash of yellowish colorings in tail and wings are distinctive.* Has loud "slee-lip" or "chee-lip" calls, a soft "it-i-lit" note, and a very buzzing "szreeeeee."

195. COMMON GOLDFINCH *(Spinus tristis).* 5-5½". Breeds from Newfoundland and southern Canada to Arkansas, northern areas of Gulf states, and northern Georgia; winters from southern border of Canada to Gulf Coast and Florida; inhabits open areas. *Small size, black wings, tail, and forehead, and yellow color in males are unique;* female is dull olive brown with white bars on black wings and has a thick bill. Very long, clear and beautiful canary-like song.

196. RED CROSSBILL *(Loxia curvirostra).* 5½-6½". Breeds from central Canada to the northern border areas of the United States, and through the

188. DICKCISSEL

♀

♂

189. EVENING GROSBEAK

♂

♀

190. PURPLE FINCH

♀

♂

191. PINE GROSBEAK

♀

♂

192. BLUE GROSBEAK

♂

♀

193. ROSE-BREASTED GROSBEAK

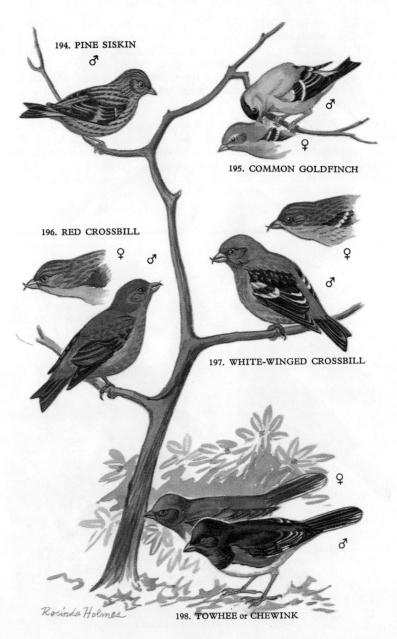

194. PINE SISKIN
♂

195. COMMON GOLDFINCH
♂
♀

196. RED CROSSBILL
♀
♂

197. WHITE-WINGED CROSSBILL
♀
♂

Rosinda Holmes

198. TOWHEE or CHEWINK
♀
♂

mountains to northern Georgia; winters spottily south into southern states. *Heavy bill with crossed points and the plain dark wings are distinctive; male with dull red over head and body. Often reveals presence by cracking sound made as it opens pine cones to get nuts.* Has hard "chip-chip" note.

197. WHITE-WINGED CROSSBILL *(Loxia leucoptera)*. 6-7". Breeds from central Canada to northern border of the United States; winters spottily to central states; frequents spruce forests. Resembles the Red Crossbill except for *white bars on wings;* it is much smaller than the similar appearing Pine Grosbeak; and young birds can be mistaken for Brownstreaked Siskins (194), but have bigger bills and no yellow. Musical "peek" note or a "shif-shif" call such as might be made by an insect.

198. TOWHEE or CHEWINK *(Pipilo erythrophthalmus)*. 7½-8½". Breeds from Massachusetts, southern Ontario, and southern Manitoba to the Gulf. Frequents open brushlands and burnt or cut-over lands, where it can be heard scratching noisily for insect food or emitting its loud "chewink!" call. *Male has distinctive black head, back, and white-edged tail, red eye, and reddish-brown sides;* in female, the black is replaced by brown.

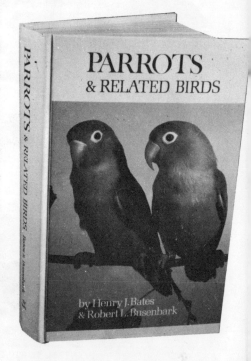